From the Door
of an Orphanage

FROM THE DOOR OF AN ORPHANAGE

The Hal Phillips Story

Pastor Hal Phillips

Printed in the United States of America by BookMasters, Inc
Ashland OH
January 2015

Rev. date: 12/29/2014

To order additional copies of this book, contact:
Xlibris
1-888-795-4274
www.Xlibris.com
Orders@Xlibris.com
651111

Contents

DEDICATION

This book is dedicated to Mom and Pop, Donald and Frances Phillips. By opening their hearts and home they gave me a chance to have a future of hope. Without their love, discipline, and guidance my life story would be so different.

INTRODUCTION

I have a story to tell you! It is a very familiar story to me because it is my story. Please let me take you back in time so you can see how God changed my life.

My life was shattered and empty until I met Jesus. As you read the following pages you will see how sin can break a family and individuals. You will also read how God can take not just one, but three children whose lives were broken and made them a part of His family and service.

As I begin to write the events of my life it is January 1986. I am serving as a pastor in the Free Methodist Church. My brother, Eddie, is a general evangelist in the Free Methodist Church. My sister, Julie, is married to a minister in the Church of Christ.

How did all three living children of an alcoholic couple find their way into God's eternal kingdom and full time Christian service?

You will find the answer to this question as you read how God took Hal Phillips "From the Door of an Orphanage."

Please note – I would like all readers to know that I hold no animosity or bitterness toward anyone as a result of the events of my life. The Lord has forgiven me and He has given me the grace to forgive others. I loved my mother and had a good relationship with her.

Acknowledgements

I wish to share my deep appreciation to my brother, Don Phillips, and his wife, Beth, for their many hours of typing this manuscript.

A special thanks to "Pop" for the hours of editing done on the original manuscript.

Pastor Hal and Kathy Phillips

CHAPTER 1

A Rough Start

My father, Harold V. Phillips Sr. was a veteran of World War II. He enlisted in the U.S. Army the day after Pearl Harbor was attacked. Shortly after his basic training, he was sent to the Aleutian Islands and served on the Island of Amchitcka for 27 months. Among his battle stars in the Asiatic-Pacific Theater of Operations was one for the Battle of Kiska. This foray on August 15, 1943, drove the last of the Japanese from the Aleutians and prevented another steppingstone from falling into place for the Japanese Empire.

After Daddy had finished his tour of duty in the Aleutians, he was sent back to the states and given six weeks of infantry training. The army then gave him a short leave before sending him to Le Havre, France, aboard the Queen Mary. He was assigned to the 347th Infantry Regiment, 87th Division of the 3rd Army under the command of General George S. Patton. He earned his Combat Infantryman's Badge in a hurry as Patton's 3rd Army raced across France toward the Rhine River Basin.

It was during Patton's drive to the Rhine that my daddy was awarded the Bronze Star Medal for Valor in action. A German machine gun nest at the top of a nearby hill opened rapid fire and had his unit pinned down somewhere along the Moselle River. He flanked the hill where the firing was coming from, caught the two machine gunners by surprise and killed them both.

In the wee morning hours of March 25, 1945, Daddy was seriously wounded when his boat crossing the Rhine River was strafed by a German Burp Gun. When the boat reached the far shore, it was discovered that only three GIs were alive and they were all in serious condition. The medics loaded the three into a returning assault boat and started back across the Rhine. In midstream the boat struck a floating log and turned sideways just as a brilliant white flare lit up above them. Another burst of machine gun fire killed the other two soldiers. Daddy was the sole survivor of the boat.

My father was sent to Brooke Convalescent Hospital, Fort Sam Houston, Texas, to recuperate from his wounds. While he was at Fort Sam Houston he was awarded the Purple Heart "For Military Merit" which was Uncle Sam's way of saying, "Thanks for shedding blood for us."

The months, weeks and days seemed to drag on forever to Daddy. Healing was a very slow process, especially after having been hit twice through the stomach, as he had been. The day finally arrived when he could go home.

He left San Antonio on November 6, 1945, Honorable Discharge in hand, with the attached Certificate of Disability and a ruptured duck insignia sewn above his right breast. The duck was an official patch of a discharged veteran. Daddy didn't even know that his unit had received the Presidential Unit Citation until he read his papers.

Civilian life just wasn't the same for the gangly kid who had overnight become an adult amid the flares and machine gun fire of mortal combat in Central Europe. His disability kept him from holding a regular job and the time on his hands soon turned to drink in his body. Later it would be revealed that Daddy was an alcoholic. He met my mother in a tavern in Newport, Arkansas.

My mother was Dorothy Florence Langston. She was the youngest of ten children born to George and Mae Langston of Tuckerman, Arkansas. Mama had little discipline in her young life and told of hanging out in beer joints when she was only 15. Grandpa Langston, an alcoholic himself, said nothing to her for frequenting the bars. She met my father one night while out drinking and shortly thereafter they were married. Mama was only 16.

Their first baby was born on September 6, 1946, a lovely little girl they named Julie. She was born 10 months after Daddy's discharge and two weeks after Mama's 17th birthday. In 1948 my sister Beverly was born, but lived only a few short hours. I, Harold Jr., was born on August 26, 1950, and was immediately dubbed "Hal" in order to distinguish me from my dad. In 1951 my sister Mary Ann was born but like Beverly, she lived only a short time. My brother Eddie completed the family. He was born October 18, 1952.

My parents weren't bad people. They just got themselves caught up in a set of circumstances and let their lives get out of control. Some of this could be blamed on Daddy's psychological problems - growing up in the army and suddenly being released on society with a disability - and of course,

Mama's undisciplined youth. They got involved with the wrong crowd in the beer joints and nightclubs, spending my Dad's disability checks on booze and setting up the freeloaders. Their drinking habits began to cause suffering for Julie, Eddie and me when we'd sometimes be left in the car outside in a nightclub parking lot. Once my Uncle Don came home on leave from the army and found me asleep on the front seat of Daddy's old Buick in the Silver Moon Club parking lot. He went inside and told him off and then took me over to my Grandmother Phillips' house for safekeeping.

The young couple came to the conclusion that taking care of three kids was too much of a burden for them, so they let Daddy's mother have Julie to care for. One day they just popped in at my Grandmother Phillips' place and dropped Julie off. Daddy even signed Julie's share of the VA pension over to his mother.

Trouble just seemed to plague Daddy and Mama. Of course, most of it was of their own making. In late 1951 my Grandpa Phillips tried to get Daddy committed to the Arkansas State Hospital for treatment of his drinking problem. He finally succeeded in getting him into the hospital, but Daddy ran off shortly thereafter. So it went throughout the year of 1952.

In late 1952, my dad rented a small house trailer and he and Mama, along with Eddie and me, lived in the cramped quarters on Beech Street in Newport, Arkansas. I was now two years old and Eddie was two months old. Julie lived with my Grandmother Phillips and was now seven.

Daddy's drinking had gradually gotten worse and he was now in the throes of alcoholism. He had begun to distrust himself and had even given people money to hold for him. He gave my Aunt Frances a considerable amount of money to hold for him. He wanted his kids to have a decent Christmas. After he gave her the money, he took me to a café to eat. Then we went back to the trailer.

Later that day, a friend came by to see Daddy, but when he knocked on the door, no one answered. He could hear a radio playing in the trailer and me crying. He rapped again very hard, nearly knocking the door from its hinges, but still no one answered. He became very apprehensive and went to get Grandpa Phillips who lived about a mile from the trailer. My grandfather called the police to break the door in. When they got inside, they found me trying to get Daddy to give me a piggyback ride. However my efforts were in vain - Daddy was dead.

Due to the unusual circumstances surrounding my father's death, his body was sent to the University Hospital in Little Rock for an autopsy. They found that the cause of his death was lobar pneumonia and acute alcoholism. Daddy had died from "total toxicity" which resulted in the paralyzing of the central nervous system, hence the pneumonia. His brain had simply stopped sending signals to the rest of his body.

Daddy was only 29 when he died. His life was so short and he was so needed by his family. Eddie, Julie and I have often wept as we've stood by the graveside of our father and wondered what it would've been like to have had a daddy. Sometimes jealousy creeps into the picture when other kids have the companionship we have so many times yearned for.

After I became a Christian I visited Daddy's grave and knelt thereby and made a special request of the Lord: "Lord, help me to do everything within my power, and Your power, to help people everywhere to be free from the power of sin, so their children won't have to grieve as I have." Everywhere Eddie and I preach we ask God to use our testimony to touch mothers and fathers with His love and grace so their lives and their families will be different from ours.

Eddie and I can't remember Christmas of 1952, and I guess it's just as well that we don't. It was a sad holiday season for a lot of people. The sadness of that long-ago year still hangs heavy over Julie, Eddie and me, and it still haunts us with a sense of loss every Christmas.

CHAPTER 2

"Big Ed"

In early 1953, after Daddy's death, Mama took Eddie and me and moved to the Langston farm. The farm was located just a mile from the Battle Axe Cemetery where Daddy was buried. There we lived with my Grandmother Langston for three years, from 1953 to 1956. It is of those days on the farm that I have my earliest memories.

It was during this time on the farm that Mama met Ed Eich. Big Ed, as Eddie and I fondly referred to him, was a big, brawny automobile mechanic with an amazing amount of strength.

I can remember Mama leaving for several days with Big Ed and when they came back she brought me a little red tractor and trailer. She also brought news that she and Ed were married. Big Ed was a good man and although he was twenty years older than Mama, the newlyweds seemed to get along very well during those first years of the marriage.

Big Ed always wore a short flat-top haircut, had a large nose and eyes that blazed when he was angry. He always wore gray or green work clothes with "Ed" over the left pocket of his work shirts. His hands always seemed dirty because of the kind of work that he did. Ed was a tough man and many nights after work he'd tell of brawls where he had defeated many foes. Eddie and I would sit with eyes wide and mouths open as our new hero would tell of his many conquests over the "bad guys."

It wasn't long after Ed and Mama's marriage in 1956 that our family moved from the Langston farm to Pocahontas, Arkansas, where Ed plied his trade for Bill Taylor, a local garage owner. Ed worked long hours repairing cars and tractors to provide a living for his new family.

We moved into a small frame house that was provided by the company Ed worked for. The house, located just 50 yards from the garage entrance, wasn't fancy and was used to store hay before our family moved in. There was no indoor plumbing, but a red hand pump on the back porch provided all the water we needed; the outhouse that sat some fifty yards behind the house was as nice as the one at Grandma Langston's. The small three room house was heated by a "potbellied" stove that kept the house very warm in the cold winter months. Ed built a bed for Eddie and me that was connected to the front wall in the living room of the house. It wasn't a fancy bed, but it was special to Eddie and me because Big Ed had built it. When told that there was no money to buy a regular bed, although there seemed to be money for other less important things, we didn't care. We liked our "homemade" bed just fine.

Ed was fun to be with and many times in the evenings he would sit by the potbellied stove and entertain us with his stories. One evening he took Eddie's baby bottle, which he sucked until he was three years old, and threw it into the stove. Eddie was very unhappy when he saw his best friend disappear in the flames! For the rest of the evening Eddie walked around with his lower lip extended and wouldn't look at Ed. By the next day, though, he was back to his old self and a little more grown up.

We took great pride in our big stepfather and often bragged to the kids in the neighborhood that he was the toughest man in town. Whenever some of these friends would meet "Big Ed" they would be convinced that we were right!

While living in Pocahontas, Eddie and I were not blessed with pets as other children, and had neither a dog nor cat. We had to settle for a pet rooster we named "Chicken Phillips." We loved this rooster and although he was not as easy to cuddle as a kitten or puppy, he became a special member of our family. Chicken Phillips was an excellent pet that never seemed to cause any problems. The only times he got into trouble were occasions when he would wander up the road and awaken the customers of the local motel. The manager came to our house more than once, his face red with anger, to complain about the crowing of the noisy rooster.

Chicken Phillips made himself at home in our family outhouse, where he roosted over one of the toilet seats. Because of the rooster's manner of roosting, he never made any messes, for which we were all thankful! One night a windstorm swept across Pocahontas and blew the outhouse over. We never saw Chicken Phillips after that. Eddie and I looked anxiously for our special friend for several days, but we finally realized he wasn't coming home. It was speculated by Ed and Mama that the rooster wasn't killed, but was so frightened that he decided to find a new and perhaps safer home. This belief did ease the pain of losing our special feathered buddy.

It was during the two years in Pocahontas that problems began to surface in our family. Mama returned to her old ways, as she turned again to alcohol and drugs. She seemed to be so preoccupied with her own addictions that she'd do anything to obtain them. When I was six years old Mama would send me to the drugstore in downtown Pocahontas to pick up prescriptions that would be charged to Ed's account.

In order for me to get to the drugstore in Pocahontas I'd have to walk several miles along Highway 67, a busy state highway. Between our house and downtown was Black River, and I'd have to cross the river bridge in order to get into town. This was a terrifying experience, as I'd find myself being sucked toward the large semi-trucks as they raced past me. I found myself clinging to the rails of the bridge, filled with fear of the traffic beside me and the dark water of the river below. In my mind I could imagine myself either being crushed by the huge trucks or fighting for my life in the cold waters of the river. All I could think of was wanting to be home with Mama where I'd be safe and secure. Yet I made this trip many times during those two years to keep my mother supplied with drugs. As an incentive, Mama gave me permission to charge toys along with the drugs to guarantee that I'd be willing to make the trips again in the future.

I wasn't dumb, but because of sporadic school attendance, a lack of help with my studies at home, and the stress of having to supply drugs for Mama, my grades were very bad. As a result I spent two years in the first grade. The experience of failing in the first grade brought me to the false conclusion that I wasn't as smart as my friends and this belief affected me for a long time.

Eddie and I were very popular in the neighborhood and were constantly on the go. It seemed that everyone knew the Phillips brothers. Eddie was very young and shy with a sad look of blue in his eyes, while I did all the talking. Between that sad look in Eddie's eyes and me smiling through my crooked teeth, we could get just about anything we wanted.

Not far from Mr. Taylor's garage, where Ed worked, was Mr. Knox's grocery store. Eddie and I would walk down the highway past the motel and hang out with our friends at the little market. One day, on the spur of the moment, we decided to try our hand at "big-time crime." We planned to go into the store and each steal something and then meet outside to divide the loot. I went in and snatched some candy and when I got to the door, there stood Mr. Knox with Eddie in hand. Eddie had stolen a mousetrap and while leaving the scene of the crime was caught. It was obvious to

Mr. Knox that I was also stealing because the "Phillips Brothers" never did anything alone. Mr. Knox gave us a stern chewing out and let us go. The kind storeowner seemed to have a soft place in his heart for us and from that day on he always referred to me as "Pete" and Eddie as "Repeat." Soon everyone in the neighborhood was calling us by our newly acquired nicknames. To this day it still remains a mystery to me why Eddie decided to steal a mousetrap when the store was filled with all kinds of goodies by which any five-year-old would be tempted.

Most of the memories of those years in Pocahontas, with the exception of the "drug running," are fond memories. When I was seven years old I made a birthday wish that my sister Julie would be able to come to visit. Eddie and I were thrilled when Julie did come to stay for two weeks that summer. That time together with our sister is one of the fondest childhood memories we have.

Another of the good memories that I have is of the Pocahontas Elementary School. One of the most exciting events of my young life took place in my second year in the first grade. I was picked to play Billy Boy in the school play! I stood in the middle of a huge circle of grinning classmates as they sang "Oh, where have you been, Billy Boy? Oh, where have you been, charming Billy?..." I'd then sing, "I have been to seek a wife, she's the joy of my life. She's a young thing and cannot leave her mother." It was a great moment for a poor kid who had failed the first grade, to be the center of attention and to hear hundreds of people applaud at the close of my performance. As my classmates slapped me on the back and congratulated me on a job well done, my self-esteem took a step up from the feelings of failure that had been so real from the year before.

It was during that second year in the first grade that I had my first fight. My best friend was a boy named Bruce. I always called him "Brucie Goosie." One day in class, Bruce and I were sitting across a table from one another when we began to argue. Bruce got so mad that he spit on me. I in turn hit Bruce square in the mouth with my first-grade fist. Bruce followed up my lip-splitting blow by picking up a sharp pencil and jabbing the leaded end into my side. The teacher broke up the mite-sized brawl and took us to the medicine room across the hall, where we received a sound spanking. Bruce and I were then told to sit in the room until we apologized to each other. Before long, we got over our anger and were laughing about our behavior. At recess no one could tell we had even argued. I still think of "Brucie Goosie" whenever I look down and see the gray mark on my side where the lead from Bruce's pencil still lies beneath my skin!

1958 was an exciting year for me, as I finally graduated from first grade after two years of hard work. When class was dismissed on the last day of school, I walked into the play yard of the elementary school I had attended for those two long years and opened my report card. When I saw that I had passed to the second grade, I took a deep breath, threw my arms into the air and let out a loud "whoopee"! I was so happy and relieved that I just hollered at the top of my lungs, so everyone would know I wasn't a flunkey anymore!

CHAPTER 3

The Junk Yard Years

In the summer of 1958 Big Ed, Mama, Eddie and I packed all our belongings and moved back to Newport. Ed had received a job offer from the Holden Motor Company to work as a mechanic in their garage near downtown Newport.

As in Pocahontas, the new employer provided a house for our family to live in as a benefit for employment. The house was located over three miles from Newport, next to the Holden Salvage yard, which was a part of the Holden family enterprise. Although the house was larger than the home we had moved from, it was a devastating place. The very sight of the house would depress most people. Tarpaper covered the exterior of the house, which had a roof covered with rusted corrugated tin. Anytime there was rain or hail, the noise of the impact on the roof was almost deafening. Some of the walls in the house had no wallpaper, and the paper on the ceiling of the living room was hanging so badly it looked as though it would fall any minute. There were places in the walls of the house where you could see through to the outside and in one bedroom some of the windows were missing. The interior of the house included four rooms and a storeroom that Eddie and I always referred to as the smokehouse. As before, there was no indoor plumbing in the house. The hand pump was beside the house and the outhouse was across a fence that separated the house from the junkyard. Surrounding the house on three sides were old junk cars and trucks that were collected and provided used parts for those in need of auto repairs. When the junkyard was full and space was needed for more wrecked cars and trucks, the Holdens would just park their extra junks in the front yard of our house. Eddie and I lived at the junkyard until the summer of 1963.

The ramshackle dwelling was a poor excuse for a house and Eddie and I would be so embarrassed when any of our friends would come around. One reason for our embarrassment was that just across the highway from the junkyard was a nice subdivision with about twenty beautiful homes where most of our friends lived. We often found our way to the subdivision to visit our schoolmates, but when our friends wanted to return the visit, we always had an excuse to keep them away from our house. Our pride just wouldn't allow us to invite our friends to see the dilapidated house with its poor furnishings. We just knew our friends would laugh when they saw the dump we lived in.

Our school bus would usually stop on Highway 67, out of sight of the house, to pick us up in the morning and let us off after school. For some unknown reason, the bus driver changed his route one-week and the bus stopped right in front of the junkyard house. When the bus driver made the turn on to our road, I began to plead with him to go another way. By the time the bus stopped in front of the junkyard, I was almost in tears. Eddie got off the bus and ran into the house, but I began to walk in the opposite direction, pretending that I lived somewhere else. When I heard the cruel laughter of my friends as they saw our house, I feared it wouldn't be the last time.

The location of the shanty wasn't the best site around, but Eddie and I tried to make the best of it. We played in the old rusty wrecked cars and pretended that we were drag racing down the highway. When we played in the wrecked trucks we would imagine we were truckers traveling across the U.S.A.

We built a tree house in a tree next to the house and sometimes we'd climb up there and pretend we were escaping wild animals in the darkest jungles of Africa. We had figured out a way to jump from the tree house onto a junk tanker truck across the fence, then on to an old dump truck, to a tractor, and so on. If we were careful, we could go almost fifty yards without ever touching the ground. In this manner the wild animals of our imaginations couldn't devour us. One day the County Health Department sent a lady to spray all the houses in the area for bugs. Eddie and I talked her into climbing up and seeing our tree house and before she got away, we had persuaded her to spray the tree house too.

In the front yard of the house at the fence line was a large walnut tree. We found a big limb, and to it we tied a long rope to which we tied an old burlap sack stuffed with rags. We'd take turns being Tarzan and swing from the giant walnut tree. Many a Tarzan yell was caught by the wind and echoed through the chambers of junk cars. The meager surroundings seemed to bring out the best of our imaginations, as we played with our makeshift toys and tried to make the best of our poverty.

In the fall of 1958, Eddie and I started school in Newport. I was now in the second grade and Eddie was starting his education career as a big first grader. We attended the East Newport Elementary School until the school was torn down two years later. I seemed to be doing a little better in school, but Eddie was running into some of the same problems that I had faced. He had a hard time grasping the subject matter and with no help at home, like me, Eddie failed the first grade.

Ed was adjusting well to his new job, but had to work long hours in order to get his work done. Although there were occasional disagreements during the first couple of years, our home life was fairly peaceful.

Our family was well cared for, especially when it came to clothing. There was plenty of clothing, but Mama refused to do any regular laundry chores. There was an old wringer washing machine that sat on the back porch of the house, and only occasionally was the sound of the loud motor and sloshing clothes heard through our home. When Eddie and I got new clothes, we'd wear them until they were too dirty to wear anymore. Many times those perfectly good clothes would be thrown into the "smokehouse" storeroom, never to be worn again. If they were washed, we'd wear the same clothes to school for a full week before changing for the next week, which meant that every day we'd wear the same shirt, pants, socks and even underwear. Other kids at school would often make fun of our "limited wardrobe," but it was a reality we learned to live with.

As the months passed, problems again began to surface in Mama's life. As before, she began to demand that Eddie and I provide her with the drugs she thought she couldn't live without. The Missouri Pacific Railroad passed just a quarter of a mile from our house and the track passed through downtown Newport, five miles to the south. Eddie and I would walk along the railroad tracks to Newport, where the drugstore sat just across Front Street from the train depot.

Sometimes we wouldn't have money to purchase the drugs. If we were fortunate, the druggist would charge the prescriptions, but when the account began to grow and no payments were made, he began to demand cash. Eddie and I would then have to resort to some special "fund-raising" activities. This would begin by finding our stepfather at his job and telling him how sick Mama was and how desperately she needed the medication. This worked a few times, but soon Ed became wise to the drug problem and refused to fund Mama's addiction. When this source dried up, we'd resort to stopping strangers on the street and pleading for money to help our "very sick" mother. Most of the time this would work but a few times we'd have to return home empty handed. This was an experience that brought fear to both of us, because when Mama didn't get the pills, she'd lose control of her senses and scream, swear, and threaten to kill herself if Eddie and I didn't "produce." Because of the fear of not getting the drugs and having to face the wrath of our mother, I decided to keep a stash as a last resort. If all else failed I could turn to this stash of drugs and believe me, I was glad they were there. If you don't think that small towns have streetwise kids, I can assure you that Eddie and I were as streetwise as any urban kid in New York City or Detroit.

One day Eddie and I were walking along the railroad tracks near the city limits of Newport. We noticed some city workers and a policeman at the dog pound, which sat next to the tracks. The policeman took out his gun and shot each of the dogs in the head and the city workers put the dead animals in dump trucks, to take them to the dump. This was one of the most shocking scenes we'd ever seen, and we pledged to do something about this awful waste of life.

A month or so later we again walked past the dog pound. It was a crude concrete structure consisting of a wall, a shaky gate and wire mesh covering the entire structure. There were more dogs that day than we had ever seen and no one else around. Eddie and I got the gate open and let all those dogs out! I've never seen a happier bunch of "pound hounds" as they were given their freedom that day.

Ed would usually work Sundays, even though it wasn't a common practice to have your place of business open on Sunday in the 1950s and early 1960s in Arkansas. He would go into the garage and work long hours. As Mama's drug and alcohol problem worsened, Ed was gone more and more. He increasingly spent more time away from Mama, Eddie and me. He began coming home later in the evenings and before long, he wasn't even coming home at night.

Eddie and I knew there were big problems and we were scared that our stepfather was going to leave for good. We often wondered out loud how we'd survive if Ed were to leave. We knew Mama wasn't capable of taking care of us with her many problems. We also knew there'd be no money for food, because Mama spent every dollar that come into the house on booze and pills.

Although we were fearful that Ed was going to leave, we couldn't really blame him. Every time he came home there was a nasty scene. We used to go to my Grandmother Langston on Sundays when Ed was still coming home. The visits would begin with a happy reunion, as several of Mama's brothers and sisters would come to the old homestead. But it wouldn't be long until the alcohol began to flow and the results were always the same. There were ugly scenes of accusations, fighting, cursing and bickering. Ed had to step in many times and break up fights that would erupt. All this would take place while my Grandmother Langston lay in her room bedridden. Many times I heard her praying and pleading with her children to stop tearing the family apart.

On one Sunday afternoon, a neighbor from a few miles down the road stopped by to show off his new pickup truck. Upon his arrival he was coaxed into drinking to his new truck and before he left the farm for home, he was drunk. Shortly after he drove off toward home, we left for Newport. Less than a mile down the road we came upon the neighbor sitting in the middle of the road crying, and not far away was his new pickup truck, flipped upside down in the ditch. He wasn't seriously injured, but the truck was a total loss.

On another Sunday during a visit at my Grandmother's, Mama got so drunk that we laid her on the floor of the backseat of the car and covered her with a blanket. We did this in case we met anyone we might know. We didn't want them to know the condition Mama was in.

When we got home that Sunday, Ed went across the junkyard to see someone. Mama was convinced that he was with another woman and in a drunken rage, took a brick and broke every window and light out on his car.

It was this type of activity that drove my stepfather out of our house. As bad as things were, Eddie and I wanted Ed to stay, even though we knew it'd only be a matter of time before he'd be gone.

Things were bad for us at that time, but little did we know that things were going to get a whole lot worse before they would get better.

CHAPTER 4

From Bad to Worse

In the fall of 1962, Eddie and I were attending the Gibb-Castleberry Elementary School in Newport. I was now in the sixth grade and doing fairly well in my studies. Although things were going better for me, Eddie was having a terrible time. Because of his learning difficulties and our bad home situation, Eddie failed the fourth grade. This was now the second time Eddie had failed and he was only in the fourth grade. This was very hard on Eddie and he began to believe he was dumb, although much of his learning difficulty had nothing to do with his intelligence.

As Eddie and I progressed through the 1962 – 1963 school year, our stepfather nearly disappeared from the scene. He worked all day and spent his nights with another woman everyone referred to as "Red." Ed would drop in about once a week for a few minutes and give Eddie and me enough lunch money to get us through the week.

Another problem arose at home as Ed started staying away at night—it was fear. Our house was old and rickety and there were no locks on the doors. One of the bedrooms didn't even have windowpanes in one of the windows. Mama had kicked out one of the windows in the living room during one of her drunken rages. As a result, we had to rush her to the Newport Hospital to have her severely cut foot stitched up. Eddie and I ashamed that passersby would see the broken window, took the windowpanes from the bedroom to replace those destroyed by my mother. There was no money to replace the bedroom windows, so we did without.

The salvage yard was not a safe place to be at night. People would roam through the rows of junk cars, looking for parts they could steal. One day I talked to two men who were removing wheels from a semitrailer. Later

Eddie and I found they stole the wheels. I had to go to the police station and try to pick them out of a lineup.

One night my Uncle Steve was staying overnight with us. When he got up early the next morning to get ready for work, he saw a man looking in the kitchen window. Mama, Eddie and I were all asleep when this took place. Uncle Steve was so startled by the "peeping tom" that he let out a yell that woke all of us up! When we went to the kitchen to see what the commotion was all about, we found him standing near the window. His face was pale and his voice trembled as he related the frightening experience to us.

Mama was not a big woman, only about 5' 2" tall and weighing no more than 100 lbs. We found little comfort in her protection. Eddie and I both knew that Mama couldn't physically control either of us. Any intruder that might break into our house could easily overcome her defenses. This reality created a strong sense of insecurity and fear in us. I recall rigging some chain locks I made from scraps I found in the junkyard to try to secure the doors.

Eddie and I coped with the fear pretty well until Mama began to leave us alone. Our greatest fear was arriving home from school and finding an empty house. Each afternoon as we walked into the yard after school, my heart would begin to pound as I imagined going into the house and finding no one home. I could imagine being left alone to take care of Eddie and myself in the dark junkyard. When Mama did leave she never left a note telling us where she was or when she'd be back. Many times it would be late at night when we'd hear a car stop and drop her off in front of the house. One time a car stopped in the yard and a man just opened the door and Mama rolled out on the ground. We didn't know if she was even alive, but soon found out that she was passed out drunk.

When Mama was not drunk or doped up, she was a nice person. Eddie and I were always excited when we'd come home from school and find Mama "in her right mind." Sometimes we'd get off the school bus and could smell the sweet aroma of a freshly baked cake. Mama knew that our favorite was a yellow cake with chocolate frosting. She could make the best one in town. These times were great, but they were few and far between. Most of the time when we got home, we'd find the beans, our main food, burning on the stove and Mama passed out in bed.

On top of the addiction of alcohol and drugs, Mama was addicted to cigarettes. She smoked several packs a day. We didn't have a mattress, couch or chair in our house that didn't have cigarette burns on it. When Mama didn't have money to buy cigarettes, she would send Eddie or me to buy a King Edward cigar. She would puff on it just enough to relieve her craving and then put it out. As a result, the cigar could last for several days.

It was with one of those King Edward Cigars that I smoked for the first time. After mama had her smoke one day, I took the half-smoked cigar and hid behind the kitchen stove. I relit the cigar on the pilot light and began to puff. The house already smelled like cigar smoke, so no one noticed my contribution to air pollution! Things were going swell until I began to feel sick and dizzy. When my stomach began doing flips, I decided that smoking was not for me. I'm thankful that I started smoking with a strong cigar, for I have never smoked since.

Each day that Ed stayed away, we found less food in the house. Many days the only food we'd have would be our school lunches. Eddie and I would ask for the leftovers from our friends' lunch trays so we'd have food at suppertime to share with Mama. It was bad enough to be hungry, but just 25 yards from our house was a little restaurant called the "Shamrock Café," which sat on Highway 67. When a breeze blew from the west, the aroma of the cooked food would drift across our small home. One day I couldn't stand this torment any longer. I went to the restaurant to see if I could get some food. A man was sitting in his car, eating a hamburger and french fries, approaching the man I told him how hungry I was and he gave me his remaining fries. I took them home to share with Eddie and Mama. It is hard to imagine, as I look back, the excitement we had as we shared that handful of french fries.

As Mama's addiction grew, Eddie and I were forced to go door to door, asking for money and rides to the drugstore. During the day we'd ride our bikes to town and beg for money on the streets. At night it was a different story. One night I had to walk to Mr. Hohn's house, about a mile down the road. Mr. Hohn drove our school bus and was a very nice man. He knew of Mama's problems and refused to give me money to buy pills. As I began the mile-long walk home I realized I was in trouble. It was a very dark night with no moon or stars in sight, and I couldn't see my hand as it moved in front of my face. Too embarrassed to ask Mr. Hohn for a ride, I started to find my way home. That was one of the most terrifying miles of my life. As I walked along, I couldn't tell if I was in the middle of the road or near one of the ditches. Several times I tumbled into the ditch as I moved too close to the edge of the road. I knew there were poisonous snakes as well as many other creatures in those ditches. I imagined them all around me as I stumbled through the darkness. As I groped through darkness, my heart felt as though it would pound out of my chest. My vision was further hampered as tears began to fill my eyes. Every noise, whether the chirping of crickets or the croaking of frogs, became more fearful to me as my imagination went wild. How relieved I was when finally I came to the top of the hill just east of our house. From there I could see the lights of the cars on the highway and I knew that I was almost home. I didn't know Jesus and his presence as we didn't attend Sunday school or church, and during that mile I was so alone and so afraid. Mama was waiting when I got home. She went into a rage when she learned that I didn't get any money and began to scream and cry. She even threatened to kill herself. The scene was bad, but it was a relief, after the experience I had just gone through. I was home safe and sound.

Mama would send us to a pay phone across the junkyard to call an ambulance to take her to the Newport Hospital, if we were unable to get drugs. We were usually instructed to tell the dispatcher that Mama was "hemorrhaging" and they would come to get her. Upon arriving at the hospital, Mama would find a way to get a shot and then the ambulance would bring her back home. There was no insurance or money, and the ambulance bills and hospital visits added up. My stepfather got the bills for these escapades and became enraged about the whole matter. One night Eddie and I called the ambulance and Ed found out about it. I guess he heard it on the scanner used by the wrecker service he worked for. Shortly after the ambulance arrived in our front yard, my stepfather drove in. He ordered the ambulance driver to leave then he proceeded to punish Mama for her actions by picking up a board and beating her with it until I thought he'd killed her. When he was finished, he left her on the ground crying and bleeding and drove away. Mama was black and blue from head to foot for days after the beating. As I stood and watched my mother being beaten, I was very angry and afraid. I wanted to help Mama by attacking my stepfather, yet I knew that he was much stronger than I, and would beat me for interfering. I felt like a coward as I heard Mama scream for help while I was paralyzed with fear. All I could do was stand crying and begging Ed to stop. Eddie and I helped Mama back into the house and helped her care for her cuts and bruises. Mama's body healed, but the emotional scars of that terrible night are still a part of all our memories.

One of the more humorous incidents that took place during those awful days involved a black family that lived about half a mile down the road. During those days in Arkansas white people didn't associate with black folks. They also didn't refer to them as black folks. One night I was desperate for a ride to Newport to get pills. I had some money, but I had no transportation and it was too dark to try to ride my bike or walk. After pleading with all the other people on our road for a ride, there was only one chance left, the black family that lived just east of us. I was afraid of black people, because of the awful stories I had heard and minimal contact with them.

In fear and bewilderment, I slowly approached their shanty of a house. They must have had ten dogs that kept barking as I approached their front door. A tall black man came to the door and welcomed me into the living room. There were several smiling faces that greeted me as I entered the room.

After I told them of my need for a ride to town, they gladly offered their help. I was so relieved that I wouldn't have to go home empty handed I wanted to hug each of them for their kindness.

But there was another problem with the arrangement. I was afraid to be seen with the black people, because I knew how many white people felt about them. As a result, I hid in the backseat of their car until we got to the drugstore, where I sneaked out of the car to get the pills and then sneaked back into the car and hid all the way home. Those people were so nice to me, and yet I was ashamed to be seen with them. I have often wondered how they felt about my actions that night.

One weekend, my Uncle Steve invited us to spend the weekend at his apartment in Newport. On Friday night Mama and Uncle Steve went to a bar a few blocks away. After several hours Eddie and I became concerned and went to see how Mama was. We found her in the bar and she was drunk! She couldn't walk. Eddie and I each took one of her arms and literally carried her from the bar and along the streets to the apartment. When we arrived at the apartment, we discovered that a man from the bar had followed us home. I knew he wasn't concerned for our safety, but thought he could take advantage of my mother in her drunken state. He very kindly offered to "take care" of Mama, if Eddie and I wanted to go to sleep. Instead I stayed awake and sat on the edge of the bed where Mama slept for nearly an hour, as he just sat and stared at me. I could tell he hated me, but I didn't care. I was determined he wasn't getting close to Mama. After a while, it seemed like days, the man left and I never saw him again.

Eddie and I only saw Mama have the DTs once, but that one time was enough for a lifetime. DTs is an abbreviation for delirium tremens, which is a violent form of delirium caused by excessive use of alcohol and drugs.

We were at my Grandma Langston's farm, and the booze had been flowing heavily all evening. When we got ready for bed, Mama began to imagine that there were snakes in the room. Eddie and I tried to persuade her that it was just her imagination, but she was convinced they were real. Then she saw spiders crawling on her, which were soon joined by the snakes. She screamed in terror and jumped around the room, trying to escape her imagined adversaries. We couldn't stand to see Mama in this maddened condition and went to sleep with our grandmother. Mama's addiction was beginning to take its toll on her and on Eddie and me as well.

The saddest thing that happened to us during those days in the junkyard was when our little brown puppy died. We loved that little dog and even though it was a stray, it was special to us. Although we loved the puppy, we found that feeding it was almost impossible. We didn't have food for ourselves most of the time, much less for a dog.

Each day we'd check on our puppy and found it was doing worse. It grew weak and sickly in spite of all the attention we gave it. Finally one day we went to the back porch and found the puppy dead. The small dog had starved to death before our eyes, and there was nothing we could do about it. Eddie and I were brokenhearted as we dug a little grave and buried our little friend. It seemed so unfair that the little dog had lived such a short time, and while it was alive it was so hungry. For weeks I would cry every time I thought of the little puppy that never had a chance. I wondered if we might face the same fate as the puppy.

With our stepfather gone, there wasn't any money for food or clothing. Much of our clothing was thrown away, rather than being washed and cared for. The rest slowly wore out. Eddie and I went to school many times wearing no socks or underwear. Once I wore Mama's underpants when I had none and was so self-conscious about it, I decided I'd rather go without than wear girls' underwear. Sometimes we'd go to school with holes in the soles of our shoes. It's no wonder the other kids used to make fun of the way we looked.

Eddie and I got so tired of going without, we began to steal. It made no difference whether it was a neighbor or a nearby store, if we saw the chance, we'd steal. We really didn't steal just to steal, we were hungry. We'd steal food or anything we could to get food. Once we found a good quantity of soda pop bottles in ditches near the highway. We redeemed them and then went back that night and stole the bottles and redeemed then again the next day to the same storeowner.

One morning as we waited for the school bus, a soda pop truck pulled up to the little restaurant where the bus picked us up. While the driver was inside filling orders, Eddie and I stole a case of pop and hid it in the bushes. We went to school and when we got off the bus that afternoon, we carried our "loot" home. We were probably the only thieves to ever use a school bus for a getaway car.

Once Eddie and I felt that our house needed to be brightened up a bit. We found a storage building not too far from our house that was left unlocked. We entered the building and discovered a variety of paints and supplies. I recall stealing several rolls of silver paper, but Eddie remembers taking buckets of silver paint. Whatever it was, we covered the walls of the living room of our broken-down house. Whether it was silver paper or paint, we both remember that people who came to visit us needed sunglasses because of the brightness!

Although we stole, if an opportunity came along for us to work, we'd jump at it. Some neighbors down the road, by the name of Hodge, had some cotton fields near our house and Eddie and I'd get an old burlap sack and pick cotton. We had to pick a hundred pounds of cotton to make three dollars. That was a full day's work.

One of the events that almost ended my brother's life had to do with money. Our cousin Pat came to spend a weekend with us at the junkyard. Pat had gotten a Friday night babysitting job at a home only half a mile from our house. When she arrived, she asked if I'd like to make some money by helping her baby-sit. I was elated with the opportunity to get some money for food and necessities.

Pat and I babysat from 6 p.m. to 3 a.m., and returned to the junkyard exhausted. I fell into bed with my clothes on and slept soundly until noon the next day. Eddie got up early that Saturday morning and decided to float a loan from me to get an old junk car running that Ed had given him. He apparently asked for my babysitting money and when I told him to leave me alone, he interpreted my response as a "yes."

When I awoke at noon, I reached into my pocket and found the four dollars I had worked so hard for was gone. Eddie had used a dollar to charge the junker's battery and spent the other three dollars for gas. The car never even started. When I found out what he had done, I was so mad I wanted to hang him from the big walnut tree in the yard. If Mama hadn't stepped in, I might have permanently damaged my dear little brother.

The conditions we were living in were becoming more unbearable every day. As we looked to the future, there was seemingly no hope for any change.

CHAPTER 5

Our First Prayer

During my year in the sixth grade, 1962 – 1963, two bright spots arose in our lives. The first was a big dog that wandered into our yard one day and decided to stay. Eddie and I fell in love with the big dog, and named him "Bigboy." This was before we had ever heard of a restaurant chain by the same name. Like the other dog we had owned, we had no food to give Bigboy, but he seemed to take care of himself.

Somewhere in this dog's past, someone had taught him to attack. All Eddie or I had to say was "sic 'em" and the big dog would go after anyone or anything. Bigboy became our constant companion, for we felt very secure when he was around. Some of the bullies who used to hassle Eddie and me now showed respect when we came around. Once a big fellow was going to beat us up, and I said, "sic 'em" and Bigboy chased him until he fled to the roof of a nearby car to escape.

Eddie and I kept a very special secret about our big dog. Although he was big and mean, he didn't have a sharp tooth in his head. He was old and his teeth had decayed. Even if he had bitten someone, he couldn't have hurt them, but we never told anyone. Everyone was afraid of our dog and that's the way we liked it, for as long as they were afraid we were safe.

The second bright spot was another pair of brothers that moved into the little town of Diaz, a mile from the junkyard. Their names were Grover and Larry Moss, and they were in the same grades as Eddie and I. The first day Grover came to school I decided it was time to show him who was boss, for even though I was skinny I could out-wrestle anyone in the sixth grade class. At recess I challenged Grover to wrestle, but in just seconds Grover was on top of me and I couldn't move. I wished I had kept my mouth shut. From that day on, Grover and I were best friends.

Grover and Larry's family had moved to Diaz from Batesville, where their father had been severely burned in a house fire. The Moss family was poor like us, and they were on welfare. Mrs. Moss was also in bad health and neither she nor Mr. Moss was able to work. In those days, the people on welfare received food in silver cans with black lettering from the government. Whenever I went to Grover's house there was always food. I can remember feeling jealous of the Moss family because, even though they were poor like us, they had food. I sometimes wished we hadn't received the Veterans Administration and Social Security checks so we could have food like Grover's family.

One Sunday afternoon, Eddie and I rode to Diaz to see our buddies. We were a little bored, so we decided to go over to Buck Hurley's tractor dealership and test-drive some tractors. We each picked a tractor, got them started, and raced them around the grain elevators next to the dealership. Things were going fine until Mr. Hurley drove by and saw us test-driving his farm equipment. He went for help and before we knew it there were five or six men chasing us through the rows of tractors and around the grain storage bins. I was hiding under a big drainpipe, scared for my life, when a big man walked up and stood maybe six inches from my head. He swore that if he ever caught us, we'd be sorry we were ever born. I don't know if he did it for effect or not, but it worked! The Phillips brothers and the Moss brothers were never seen near Mr. Hurley's tractors again.

Eddie and Larry did get into trouble with the State Police shortly after the tractor incident. Larry came over to visit Eddie one afternoon and they went to the County Garage, next to the highway, to play on the piles of sand and stone. While there they discovered a car, which belonged to one of the workers, with the keys in the ignition. They proceeded to start the car and drive it around the area, which was completely fenced in. After a while, the workers came back from their road duties and chased the boys. Eddie drove the car into a gravel pile and both boys fled on foot. The workers called the State Police and a search followed, but Eddie and Larry had escaped. Later Eddie took Larry home on his bike. Instead of taking the back roads to Larry's house in Diaz, Eddie rode down the highway directly in front of the State Police Post. One of the troopers spotted the boys and chased them down. The two ten-year-olds got a good chewing out and a firm warning to stay out of trouble or else!

Eddie and I never went to church. I was twelve and had only been in a church building once, for my Grandfather Phillip's funeral, and I don't recall that Eddie had ever attended a church service. Grover and Larry attended the Baptist Church in Diaz occasionally and invited Eddie and me to go with them. We wanted nothing to do with church, but when we found out that we could attend a party on Saturday night if we attended church the Sunday before, we decided to give it a try.

We decided to attend the Sunday evening service because the crowd wouldn't be as large and frightening to us. We sat in the back row on the right side of the sanctuary so we could make a speedy exit when the service was over, but we didn't realize just how speedy our exit would be.

We had no idea how to act in such surroundings and were totally unfamiliar with everything that was going on. When Rev. Kent stood up to preach I was embarrassed, because I had beaten his son Mike up many times on the school bus. Rev. Kent preached on the subject of "hell" that night. Eddie and I were so spiritually ignorant we didn't know that hell was a bad place. We just thought hell was a cussword so we were convinced that Rev. Kent was swearing. Every time the preacher would say "hell," Eddie and I started giggling. After several episodes of loud laughter, the pastor stopped his sermon and asks us to leave the church. The first time Eddie and I attended a regular church service we were thrown out, because we were so noisy. But we did attend the party and had a great time.

The only bible that we had in our house was a Gideon New Testament. I received it when I was in the fifth grade at Gibb-Castleberry Elementary. Some well-dressed men came to the school one day and gave all the kids in our class a beautiful little New Testament. I was so proud of that little bible and read it often. It was the first bible I ever owned and I believe it planted the first seeds of God's Word in my heart that later grew to eternal life for a poor kid who needed Jesus.

Although I didn't go back to the church, Grover and I had a little service one day in a field near our house. We drew a cross in the dirt and I recited a small part of the Lord's Prayer I had heard on television. Grover knew a couple verses of a song, so we sang a little and closed with the Catholic sign of the cross. Although we had no religious training I could sense a deep desire to draw close to God.

A few days after our "worship service" Eddie and I found that we were once again left alone in the dark junkyard, and the fear was more than we could bear. I turned to Eddie and said, "Let's pray and ask God to help us." We bowed our heads and prayed. I remember asking God, "What have we done God, to deserve this awful life we are living? Please help us! Please help us! Do something so we won't have to live this kind of life any longer." I don't know why, but after we prayed this prayer, we threw in that we'd also like a little brother. We never imagined that this prayer would be answered, but in time, God would answer our prayer. The loving, caring

God to whom we'd poured out our hearts would grant even the request for a little brother, which seemed impossible because Mama could have no more children.

In our hearts we were hoping that God would immediately answer our prayers, but it wasn't to be. Within a few days of the first real prayer that Eddie and I prayed, I came home to find that Mama had attempted suicide by cutting her wrists. When I saw Mama in the bed with blood pouring from her slashed wrists, I became hysterical and ran around the house screaming, "My mother's dead, my mother's dead." I ran for the pay phone at the junkyard office and called my stepfather. He, in turn, called an ambulance, which rushed Mama to the hospital where her wrists were stitched up.

After this incident, I began to give up hope that God or anybody else could do anything to help Eddie and me. It seemed that my life had reached rock bottom. Little did I know that the summer months that were approaching would be so traumatic as to alter the course of our lives in a dramatic way.

Chapter 6

My Long Hot Summer

In June of 1963, I graduated from the sixth grade and Eddie finished his second year in the fourth grade. I didn't realize as I entered the summer months that this would be the worst summer of my twelve years and possibly my entire life.

It began when my stepfather filed for divorce at the beginning of the summer. He and his new woman, Red, were now living together and the only time Eddie and I saw him was when we'd visit the garage where he worked, or see him on the street. Eddie and I missed him very much, for with his leaving the traces of stability disappeared from our home.

Mama persuaded her brother Steve to move in with us. He worked at the Victor Metal Plant just across the road from our house, and this was a convenient location, as he could walk to work each day. The only problem with having Uncle Steve live with us was that he too was an alcoholic.

Uncle Steve had a good job and would receive good pay each week, but almost all of his money was spent on alcohol. He would get a ride to Newport on Friday nights and go to "Tom's," a little bar on Beech Street, where he met his friends and drank. At about midnight, a taxicab would pull into our yard and Uncle Steve would get out with a sack of groceries, which was his rent payment, a case of beer and maybe ten dollars in his pocket. He and Mama would stay up and drink the case of beer, unless they passed out first. This same series of events was repeated every Friday night as long as Uncle Steve lived with us.

Eddie and I, scoundrels that we were, would be up early Saturday morning to take our spoils. We'd crawl under the rollaway bed where Uncle Steve slept and steal some of the money left in his wallet. We knew that

Uncle Steve took his wallet, placed it in a paper sack and stuck it under his mattress. By crawling under the bed we could reach through the wires of the support, cut through the paper bag with a sharp knife, and take out the wallet. We never took enough to raise suspicions and never were caught.

By Monday, all the groceries and money were gone. The rest of the week we had to somehow make do any way we could. In the summer months there were no school lunches to see us through, and our hunger became more intense. Once we were so hungry that we mixed some old flour we found in one of the cupboards with water and made patties that we cooked on the stove. This was all we had to eat for almost a week. It was bad enough not to have food, but the aroma of food from the nearby restaurant continued to drift toward our house. The aroma served as a constant reminder to us that there was plenty of delicious food just out of our grasp.

When we got a social Security or V.A. check, Mama would cash the check, buy a few groceries and spend the rest on drugs or alcohol. Mama's drug problem was getting so serious that Eddie and I were afraid for her life. There were times when we'd have to call an ambulance to come and get Mama and take her to the hospital. Before she went just to get a shot, but now it was to save her life. Now we were afraid that one day we'd come home and find Mama dead from an overdose or another suicide attempt.

Eddie and I continued to supply drugs for Mama, and were now finding ourselves responsible for providing food for the three of us as well. We would leave the house at 7 a.m. and be gone all day and half the night, and we never had to explain where we were. We were totally undisciplined because our mother couldn't even control her own life, much less ours. I became convinced that the only reason she kept us around was to supply her habit.

One hot summer afternoon, Eddie and I came home to find an awful mess. Mama was lying in bed unconscious, either from drugs or alcohol or a combination of both. She had been smoking and the mattress had caught fire and was smoldering. We were terrified when we discovered that we couldn't wake Mama up and were convinced that she was dying. We called for an ambulance, which arrived in just a few minutes. The ambulance attendants were very concerned about mama and rushed her to the Newport Hospital.

After the ambulance left for the hospital, Eddie and I dragged the smoldering mattress out into the backyard and doused it with water from the hand pump nearby. Eddie rode into town on his bike, while I checked to make sure nothing else was burning. When I had checked around and was convinced all was back to normal, I headed to Newport on my bicycle to see how Mama was doing. On my way to the hospital I passed through Diaz, where Grover lived. I decided to stop and ask Grover to go to the hospital with me. I needed someone to give me some encouragement and strength.

When I got to the hospital, I was surprised to see my Uncle Steve standing outside the emergency room entrance. As I was getting off my bike, he walked over and asked, "Hal, how did it burn?" I stood there in silence, because I didn't know what he was talking about. He waited a moment, then asked me again, "How did it burn?" I looked at him with a puzzled look and asked, "How did what burn?" His answer was somewhat louder, "The house, it burned to the ground!" Apparently I hadn't gotten the smoldering mattress completely out and the fire had spread, destroying our house. I just stood there and shuddered. A shock wave went through my body like a wave from a giant ocean. Everything was gone except my bike and the dirty clothes I had on. You'll never know how it felt to have absolutely nothing except the bike I rode to town and the dirty clothes I had on. Everything was gone.

As I entered the hospital lobby still dazed from the news I had just received, I heard Mama screaming, "My baby is dead. My baby is dead!" I followed her voice and found her in the emergency room with several doctors and nurses trying to restrain her. I found out that when Eddie had arrived at the hospital earlier she had sent him back to the house to get her "pills." Now she had just been told that our house had burned and she was sure that Eddie had died in the fire. Could it be true? Was Eddie dead? I was terrified! In my mind I could see Eddie crying out in the flames. He was the closest person in my life. How could I lose him? What would I do without Eddie? I wanted to run from the hospital to find him.

Julie arrived at the hospital within minutes. She had received word of the fire and learned that Mama was there. We stood hand in hand as we waited to receive some news of Eddie's whereabouts. We wanted to go to the house, but were persuaded that our mother needed to know we were safe and it was best to stay with her.

The anxiety of those moments was broken when Eddie, his eyes wide with panic, came running through the emergency room door. When I saw my brother my heart leaped in my chest! I was so glad to see him I wanted to hold him and just cry for joy. He was alive and I was so thankful. He told us that when he arrived home, the house was in flames. He stayed until the fire was out and then headed back to town. He had no idea that we were concerned for his safety and was surprised by the demonstration of excitement at his appearance.

Although the crisis of Eddie's safety was past, we still had to deal with other problems created by the fire and its destruction. A later search of the remains of our house found that only the barrel of my stepfather's shotgun was salvaged. The greatest loss to me was our family picture collection and my dad's Army uniform, which I cherished.

Julie took Eddie and me home to my Grandmother Phillips' house, where we stayed for several weeks. My grandmother, whom we always called Nanny, had been concerned about Eddie and me for a long time, but because of the strained relations between her and Mama, we didn't get to see her or Julie often. Nanny called the local radio station and asked for donations of clothes, and within a few hours Eddie and I had more clothes than we'd ever remembered owning before. Nanny had to make another call to the station the next day, to thank everyone for their donations and to request that no more clothes be brought. We had no room to store them.

Nanny lived in a duplex on Newport Avenue next to the City Park, which was quite different than the junkyard we'd been used to. She had running water, an indoor bathroom, and the biggest bathtub I'd ever seen. Eddie and I felt that we'd become rich overnight. It wasn't long before I felt almost thankful that our old shack of a house burned.

Mama remained in the hospital in Newport for about a week. One day I went to see her and I overheard my Uncle Steve and Uncle George, Mama's youngest brother, talking outside the hospital. They were saying that Mama was told she had to get serious drug treatment or she was going to die. Within a few days Mama was transferred to the State Hospital at Benton, Arkansas, for treatment of drug and alcohol abuse. Eddie and I wondered if we'd ever see Mama again as she told us goodbye just before leaving for the Benton Hospital, but in just a few weeks she was back in town.

Within days of our arrival at her home, Nanny began court proceedings to take custody of Eddie and me from my mother. She had asked Eddie and me if we wanted to stay with her, and we told her we did. We didn't want to go back to the awful existence we had known, yet at the same time we missed Mama very much. We were so torn, we loved being with Julie and Nanny, and at the same time we felt Mama needed us and we didn't want to abandon her. Emotionally we were confused; we didn't know what to do.

Nanny tried to keep us as busy as possible until school started, so we were enrolled in the Little League Baseball program and were assigned to teams. The season had started but we were put on teams anyway. I had never played baseball before, and didn't know how to catch a ball or swing a bat. The other kids on my "Case Tractor" team gave me a hard time as I struck out time after time, and misplayed the baseball almost every time it was hit to me. Then one day, with two strikes on me, I swung wildly and connected with the ball. I was as shocked as everyone else was, but I ran with all my heart, circling the bases for my first home run! When I got to home plate all my teammates met me with handshaking, slaps on the back and words of praise. It was one of the most exciting moments in my life. I will always remember my first home run.

One day Nanny sent me to the store to pick up a few groceries and when I came out of the store my stepfather and Mama were waiting for me. Mama gave me a long emotional speech about how she was now well, and she and Ed were going to get back together, and everything was going to be different. I hesitated, but got into the car with them, and we went to Nanny's to pick up Eddie and our clothes. Mama knew if she could get me to go, Eddie would follow, and that's exactly what happened. Nanny and Julie were very upset when we decided to leave, but at that time they had no legal power to keep us from going. Eddie and I packed our clothes, got into the car, and traveled to my Grandmother Langston's farm, where we took up residence. I had such high hopes for our "new beginning" and I dreamed of a happy home like many of my friends and classmates had. To my great disappointment, those dreams were short-lived; Mama returned to her old ways within days of our reunion.

Uncle George, who was an alcoholic, Aunt Bun and Mama decided to go to Newport the next week to get some pills and booze. Mama wrote a hot check at a liquor store, bought the drinks and then headed for the drugstore. Mama's doctor, who had sent her for treatment for drug addiction, had neglected to cancel her standing prescription for the drug to which she was addicted. Her downward spiral began that day and slowly but surely, Mama moved back into the same condition she was in before the fire. Again Eddie and I were caught in the middle of chaos and turmoil.

Ed came around a couple of times, but when he saw how Mama was again turning back to the dope, his visits stopped. I just knew the marriage was over this time and I couldn't blame Ed for leaving. I wanted to go with him, but I knew I couldn't.

Mama's addiction again reached proportions that demanded she be closer to her "sources," so we moved back to Newport, where my Uncle Steve had an apartment. The apartment was located in an alley just off the main highway through town. It was a small apartment with one bedroom, a kitchen, a bathroom and a small living room. My Uncle Steve, his daughter Peggy, her husband and three children, a man named Charlie, Mama, Eddie and I were all cramped into those four small rooms. I found the condition almost unbearable. The apartment was infested with thousands of cockroaches that crawled on the walls, ceilings, counter and even the table from which we ate. On top of the deplorable living conditions, all the adults in the apartment drank heavily and someone was always drunk.

Ed came to the apartment in early August to bring Mama the papers declaring that their divorce was final. Mama begged him not to leave, but he walked out of the apartment, got into his car and backed out of the alley. Mama ran from the apartment, screaming and crying in an attempt to stop Ed. She chased the car, grabbed the bumper and was dragged down the alley until she could hold on no longer. I felt so sorry for Mama as she lay in the alley crying like a baby. Eddie and I went to her to assure her of our love and helped her back into the apartment where we attended her scrapes and bruises.

The stress of all that was happening around me was taking its toll on me. I was twelve years old and a nervous wreck. My hands shook as if I was freezing and my fingernails bled from the constant nervous chewing. Without proper nutrition and unable to sleep at night, I began to feel weak and sick. Another symptom that appeared in my life was an onslaught of nightmares. Every night I had awful nightmares that haunted me for several years. I dreamed that I was given a totally impossible task to perform and if I didn't do it, I would be beaten or die. In one dream I was ordered to eat a mattress from a bed, with death as the penalty for failure. My life was so hopeless, and my lack of strength to handle the pressures was showing up in my dreams.

One morning a few days after Ed's visit, my Uncle George showed up at the apartment for a visit. He was very depressed because his luck had gone so bad. At one time Uncle George had been a very wealthy man. He had owned the most popular nightclub in that part of Arkansas, with such stars as Elvis Presley and Johnny Cash performing for him. He had been married to a beautiful woman and had a lovely home. All this was lost to gambling and drinking and now Uncle George had nothing.

Uncle George was a childhood hero to Eddie and me. He always took time to play with us and would take the blame if we did something stupid. I would do anything for my favorite uncle. That day, he asked me to go to a little market down the street with him. When we got to the market, he asked the owner if he would loan him some money and we walked back to the apartment. Later that day, he hitchhiked back to my Grandmother Langston's farm. I learned later that just before leaving Newport, Uncle George had purchased a large quantity of sleeping pills and alcohol to take home with him.

The day after my Uncle's visit, I decided to look up my stepfather, to see how he was doing. I went to the garage where he worked but he had already quit for the day. I knew of a bar where Ed would stop in occasionally after work; so I decided to see if I could spot his car in that area. Just as I approached the bar, I saw his car driving away down another street, so I tried to catch him. I pedaled my bicycle as hard as I could for several blocks, doing everything I could to get his attention. Finally, he looked in his rearview mirror, saw me in hot pursuit, and pulled his car over to wait for me. When I stopped next to his car, he was sitting on the fender with a big smile on his face, very pleased to see me. I had so much to talk about, but as I began to speak, I started coughing and could not stop. We were just across the street from the Newport Hospital, so Ed just picked me up in his arms and carried me to the emergency room entrance. There a nurse took me into a treatment room, where a doctor examined me. The doctor told Ed that I had pneumonia in both lungs and that I would have to stay in the hospital. I was so exhausted from all the turmoil going on in my life that I slept all night and most of the next day.

Eddie came to see me the next afternoon. I felt like a king as I got all this attention from the doctors, nurses, my stepfather, and now my brother. Eddie and I went for a walk to the lobby of the hospital, which was on the same floor I was on. As we entered the lobby area, we saw a man being brought in through the emergency entrance on a stretcher. Just out of curiosity we decided to get a little closer. As the attendant pushed the stretcher past us on the way to the emergency room, we were shocked to discover it was Uncle George. I will never forget seeing him lying there on that stretcher. He had only a ragged pair of jeans on and when he breathed, it sounded like a deep groan rather than normal breathing.

It was only a matter of minutes until Mama and several of her brothers and sisters arrived at the hospital to await any news from the doctors. Mama told me that Uncle George had been asleep for days; he was thought to have consumed a lot of alcohol and was just sleeping it off. Then someone found an empty pill bottle next to his bed and realized that he had attempted suicide.

The doctor came to the waiting room a little while later and told the family that he had pumped Uncle George's stomach, but got almost nothing. The drugs were already in his system and only time would tell whether he would live or die. It was not long until news came from intensive care that Uncle George was dead. He was the next to youngest of the ten Langston children; only Mama was younger, yet he was the first to die.

That was an awful time for Mama's family. None of Uncle George's brothers or sisters knew Jesus or the hope of eternal life. I will never forget the hopeless feeling that filled every activity for the next several days. There was almost constant weeping and wailing from family members as they mourned the loss of their brother.

The Dillinger Funeral Home, where Uncle George's funeral was to take place, was directly across the street from the hospital, so I asked my doctor if I could go to the funeral service. He agreed, but said I would have to come back as soon as the graveside service was over.

The scene was tragic, as the brothers and sisters prepared for the service to begin. Uncle Dewey and Uncle Steve brought their wine bottles, which were passed freely from person to person. Mama took Eddie and me to the casket to say goodbye to our hero. I remember her telling us that we would never see him again and that she wanted to send something with him. She reached into her purse and took out a compact makeup kit and slid it into the casket next to Uncle George's body. Mama knew nothing of the hope that Christ brings nor the comfort of the Holy Spirit.

When the minister started the service, he mentioned that he went to high school with Uncle George and that my uncle had been his idol. He told of how he used to try to have the same kind of car as Uncle George, date the same girls, and wear the same kind of clothes. Then he pointed at the casket, which sat in the same room in which my dad's casket sat eleven years before, and spoke of a wasted life of alcohol and drugs. I have never forgotten the message that day and the challenge the preacher gave to follow Christ and not waste the lives God had given us.

I returned to the hospital that afternoon to complete my two-week stay. During that time, the only time Mama came to see me was when Uncle George was brought in. Eddie and Julie came to see my stepfather and me almost daily, and Nanny came by occasionally, but Mama came only one time. I was hurt that Mama was so unconcerned about me. Every day I waited anxiously to see her face and to hear her say, "I love you, Hal," but it never happened. At the end of each day, I felt abandoned by Mama. I was so worried and thought she must be very sick or she would be there caring for me. But when Eddie visited, he informed me that Mama was not sick but just too busy. I became very angry and said I was glad she did not come, yet I wanted to see her so badly.

After two weeks, I was feeling much better and stronger. I was excited, for just a few days away was August 26, my birthday. This was not just any birthday, but my thirteenth, and I was going to be a teenager. Mama promised me a birthday cake and a party. I just knew that this would be a great day for me. Early on the morning of the 26th, I went to visit Julie and Nanny, for they too had promised me birthday presents. When I arrived back at the apartment in the early afternoon, expecting a cake, gift, and party, I found a disappointing scene. Mama, Uncle Steve, and the three adults living in the apartment were all drunk. There was no cake, gift, or party - just passed out drunks lying everywhere. I could not understand where Mama had gotten the money to buy the booze. The money was tight and I was told that a cake and small gift were all she could afford. Yet there were empty beer and whiskey bottles everywhere, and there was another sack full of unopened bottles on the kitchen table. I knew Mama had come up with some money somewhere and I wanted to know where. I awakened her and asked where she got the money for booze. She would not answer. I persisted until she knew I was not going to leave her alone until she told me. The she told me that she and Uncle Steve had gone to a hockshop and hocked some U.S. Savings Bonds my dad had bought for Eddie and me before he died. When Mama told me what they had done, it was as though something inside me snapped. I was enraged about the bonds, the party, the lack of hospital visits, the fire, and so many other things that had happened. I told Mama that I hated her. I swore at her and told her that I hoped she burned in hell. Then I walked from the apartment, slamming the door as hard as I could. I could hear Mama screaming for me not to go, but I got on my bicycle and rode from the alley.

I immediately went to Nanny's house and in tears, I told her all that had happened. I asked if I could live with her and promised no matter what, I would not go back to Mama. She and Julie welcomed me with open arms of love and a spirit of determination to do something about our plight. Eddie came later that afternoon and it was over a year before we saw our mother again.

At the time my thirteenth birthday seemed very disappointing, but as I look back now, I received some very special gifts. Eddie and I received a new family, a new home, and a new start in life. In reality, my summer of tragedy was the doorway through which I could move to a new life.

CHAPTER 7

From The Door of an Orphanage

When Julie heard of my disappointing birthday, she told me she was going to make me a special surprise. The next day she showed me a beautiful cake that had six layers. It was an unusual cake, for each layer was a different color. I told Julie that I was so hungry I could eat the whole cake. She told me if I could eat it I could have it! For the first and last time in my life, I sat and ate a six-layer cake. I ate the whole thing! It was several days before I got over the discomfort of my "bulging belly," but I will never forget my sister's beautiful six-layer cake.

Almost immediately Nanny began working to get custody of Eddie and me. She had begun the process once, but had abandoned her efforts when we went back to Mama. This time, however, we assured her she need not worry that we were going to leave. Neither Eddie nor I had any desire to go back to our old life.

One morning Nanny and Julie took Eddie and me to the county courthouse to meet with a judge. He asked us many questions about Mama and the way she had treated us. I was very honest with the judge, allowing my bitterness toward my mother to express itself. I told him how Mama left us alone, spent our money on booze and dope, and how she burned our house. We went into detail about the times of starving, and the drug running we had done for years. As we talked, the judge just shook his head as he listened to the awful tale we shared with him.

The next week there was a hearing to decide if we would remain in Mama's custody or legally be in Nanny's care. Nanny and Julie went to the hearing while Eddie and I waited anxiously at home to hear the judge's decision. When Nanny and Julie returned they were rejoicing, for Nanny was now our legal guardian. Eddie and I were so relieved when we found that we never had to go back to Mama and our old life. The only part of the hearing that disappointed us was that Mama did not show up to fight for us. She never called, she never wrote, and she sent no one in her place - she did nothing. We were very hurt when we learned of Mama's absence. I could feel my bitterness growing inside of me, as I thought that Mama did not even take time to fight for her two sons. It was the same old story as when I was in the hospital and so many times before. Mama just did not care.

A major hurdle had been overcome by the court decision, but there were so many other problems to overcome. The greatest problem was the undisciplined life we had lived for so long. Eddie and I were wild and in great need of a very strong hand. Nanny and Julie did their best, but Nanny was nearly seventy years of age and Julie was seventeen. Neither of them was strong enough to corral and tame the two wild mustangs that were now a part of their household.

Eddie and I would take off on our bikes and never tell anyone where we were going or when we would come home. One day we went to the garage where our stepfather worked and he persuaded us to go home with him to meet his new woman, Red. We spent the afternoon with them, went swimming, and had a very nice afternoon. We arrived home near evening to find Nanny and Julie beside themselves with worry. They were ready to call the police when we rode into the yard. They were glad to see that we were okay, but chewed us out and gave us a good spanking for taking off without permission.

Eddie and I were terrible liars. We lied about everything, but it was easy to see through us. I was always the one to finally break down and tell the truth. However, Eddie was so hard that he would ridicule me for being a sissy until I would beat him up to show him who was still boss.

Not far from Nanny's house was a levee that surrounded Newport to protect it from the occasional floodwaters of White River. On that levee was a great bike jump, and Eddie and I went there often. We would push our bikes to the top of the levee, ride our bikes down the steep incline, and fly up the jump at the bottom of the hill. Our bikes would fly through the air for thirty to forty feet before coming back to earth.

Eddie decided one day that he would like to try the jump on my bike. My bike was my prize possession, and I was reluctant to allow him to try. He finally persuaded me. He did fine until he hit the jump. That was when he and my bike parted company. Eddie landed with a "plop" and my bike landed with a "crash." When I got to the bottom of the hill, Eddie was just picking himself up. He was bruised and broken, but I was not concerned about him; I was worried about my bike. When I saw the bent handlebars, twisted seat, and scraped paint, I attacked Eddie and struck him several times with my fists. When I felt he had been punished enough, I took my battered bike and headed home. Eddie came along a little while later. When Nanny treated his wounds, it was hard to tell which bruises were from the bike wreck and which were from my fists. To this day Eddie still reminds me of the day when he was an accident victim and instead of helping him up, I beat him up.

Something very unusual about our new home was church attendance. Every Sunday, Julie would take Eddie and me to the First Baptist Church in Newport for Sunday school and worship. Eddie liked going to church more than I did, because he was sweet on the pastor's daughter. He even got to where he wanted to go to church on Sunday nights. I would have been worried, except for the fact that I knew he was in love. The experience of going to church was totally new to us. My sister always sat with us and told us what to do when we were confused. With her help, we never got kicked out for being noisy.

One Sunday morning as the pastor finished the service; he stepped down on the floor in front of the pulpit and invited anyone who would like to join the church to come forward. I almost fainted when Eddie pushed past me and stepped into the aisle. I thought maybe he had to go to the bathroom, but when he walked to the front of the sanctuary and shook hands with the pastor, I could not believe my eyes. Later he told me that he did it for his girlfriend, and dared me to do the same thing the next Sunday.

I realized that Eddie did not make any kind of commitment or get "saved," but his dare bothered me. I never turned down a dare, not even the time some friends dared me to light a firecracker and let it explode in the pocket of my blue jeans. Later I secretly wished that I had passed on that dare as I nursed my burned leg back to health, yet I still was proud that I had taken the dare. Now I was faced with a crisis. Would I take Eddie's dare and make a complete fool of myself or pass on it and appear to be afraid?

When we got up the next Sunday, I was determined to take Eddie's dare and walk up the aisle at the close of the worship service. But as I sat in my Sunday school class, my stomach began to churn as a result of my nervousness over the whole matter. By the time Sunday school was over, I could not even look toward the sanctuary. Instead, I walked out of the building and went home. Nanny was surprised to see me and asked me what was wrong. I just told her I was sick; which I really was, for I had just failed to take a dare for the first time I could remember. A few weeks later,

Eddie was baptized and taken in as a member of the church, although he really did not understand what it was all about.

Although Eddie was a member of the Baptist Church and I was a regular attendee, there seemed to be no change in our behavior. We were constantly into some kind of trouble and Nanny was having an increasingly difficult time handling us. She would give us a switching, which was her favorite corporal punishment, and fifteen minutes later, we were in trouble again.

In September of 1963, Eddie and I started back to school. I was attending the seventh grade at the Newport Junior High School. Eddie was in the fifth grade at the Gibb-Albright Elementary School. We were constantly in some kind of trouble and our grades were bad. When we brought home our first report cards, Nanny found that we were doing very poorly. Instead of disciplining us for our very poor grades, she gave us praise for doing as good as we did. I can still remember expecting a switching, but getting a big hug instead. Nanny could not stand my mother and placed most of the blame for our poor grades on her. Eddie and I just ate this up, realizing that we did not have to study for good grades because bad grades were acceptable to two boys who "had been through all that we had been through."

Our grades went from bad to worse, as did our behavior. Nanny was increasingly aware that by bringing Eddie and me to her home, she had taken on a task that she could not handle. She began to talk to Eddie and me about the possibility of going to an orphanage. I do not know if she was trying to scare us into following her guidelines or if she was really serious. Whatever the case, the thought of an orphanage scared us, and we were constantly pondering our future.

Nanny had been under a lot of stress since Eddie and I had come to live with her three months before. The house we lived in was a duplex with one bedroom. She and Julie slept on the couch and gave us the bedroom, which caused much congestion. It was a bad situation that was only getting worse.

On Thanksgiving Day, Nanny made a big dinner for Julie, Eddie, and me. I came walking through the kitchen and saw a pan filled with cornbread dressing ready to be put in the oven. As I saw the pan of dressing, I commented that it looked like pig slop. I felt badly for what I had said, especially after Nanny began to cry and walked out of the house, saying repeatedly that she could not take it anymore.

Julie was very upset with Eddie and me, and gave us a royal chewing out for our terrible behavior and lack of respect. She then demanded that I go apologize to Nanny. I did not like what Julie said, but I knew she was right. I found Nanny sitting next to Newport Lake, just a block or so from the house. I told her I was sorry and persuaded her to come back home with me. Although this crisis seemed to be behind us, I knew it was only a matter of time before Eddie and I would be moving on. I could not get the orphanage out of my mind, for I was becoming more and more convinced that would be our next stop.

Shortly after Thanksgiving, Nanny called a family meeting. She had a special announcement! I just knew we were going to be sent to the orphanage and the announcement would concern the details of our departure. When Nanny had us all sitting and attentive, she told us that she had been in contact with my Uncle Donald and Aunt Frances, and they had agreed to take Eddie and me into their home.

Uncle Donald was my dad's brother. He and Aunt Frances lived in Flint, Michigan, where Uncle Donald worked in a General Motors factory. They had a beautiful home and felt that they wanted to give us a chance to have a real family, including a mother and father figure. Nanny also announced another fact about my Aunt and Uncle that brought great delight to Eddie and me. They had a six-year-old son named Donny who would soon be the little brother that Eddie and I prayed for when we lived in the junkyard. As I thought about the events that were taking place, I realized God had heard the prayer of two desperate little boys and was now answering that prayer. We were excited about moving to a new home with a new family. I breathed a sigh of relief and pushed the worry about the orphanage from my mind. Uncle Donald and Aunt Frances were to come to get us at semester break in January. We would travel over 800 miles through five states to a new home and city that we had never seen before with people we did not know. I did not remember my Uncle Donald at all and only remembered meeting Aunt Frances once when she was visiting Nanny. We had never seen Donny, which added more mystery to the situation.

There was one big event that took place before Eddie and I would leave Nanny and Julie. Christmas was only a few weeks away and my sister and grandmother were determined to make it the best Christmas we had ever had. Nanny had a beautiful tree, which was covered with large blue lights, and each day the pile of presents under the tree grew, until it seemed there was room for no more.

On Christmas morning I could not believe my eyes, as I entered the living room to discover almost twice as many presents as had been there the night before. It was so exciting to be able to open present after present when we had been so used to so few presents in the Christmases of the past. Nanny and Julie had gone all out, and it was by far the best Christmas Eddie and I had ever had.

Before we knew it, 1963 slid past and the New Year was upon us. My imagination was in full gear since Nanny announced our big move to Michigan. I tried to picture the new home, neighborhood, school, and people I would soon become a part of. Eddie and I were full of questions for Nanny and Julie about our new family and although they told us as much as they could, it was never enough.

We did not realize that in just a few days, we would move not only to a different state, but a new life in almost every way. It was a change that was to be so good, yet so hard!

CHAPTER 8

A New Home

Our last day of school in Newport was an exciting day, as all my friends and teachers had special words of appreciation and farewell. Each of my teachers had to fill out a special evaluation, which I have kept through the years. My grades were not good. I had an "F" in one class, but it was changed to a "B" before anyone saw it. The "F" was easy to change, but it was not so with the "D's" since all I could do was add a "+" to them, but for a boy "who had been through all I had been through," it did not seem too bad.

The nineteenth of January was the big day. The long wait to become acquainted with our new family was finally over. Into the driveway late on Friday afternoon pulled a little white Chevrolet Corvair with three people inside. Eddie and I stood on Nanny's big porch with eyes wide to see our new family.

When they emerged, I noticed that my Uncle was not much taller than me. He was losing his hair and looked very stern. My Aunt was almost as tall as my Uncle, had thick curly hair and a big smile. My cousin Donny was little, skinny, and had a big cowlick in the front of his hairline. My immediate evaluation was that this was a great looking family. They all came in and a time of reunion and sharing took place until bedtime.

One of Eddie's friends, a boy by the name of Gib Ponder, came by during the evening to bring us a gift and say goodbye. After he left, we opened our gifts and found two one-pound boxes of chocolates. Eddie ate a few of his and decided to save the rest, but not me: like the birthday cake Julie had made me, I ate the whole box before I went to bed.

The next morning we were up early, loaded the car, and left for Michigan. I will never forget the feelings I experienced that morning. It was sad saying goodbye to Nanny and Julie because I loved them so much. I was lonely as I looked around at the town I was born in and realized I might never live there again. I felt afraid as Eddie and I started on a trip to a new world for us. Most of all, I felt sicker than a dog from eating that one-pound box of chocolates the night before. As a matter of fact, I was so sick that I rode almost all day with my face by an open window just in case! We traveled all day on Saturday in an attempt to get home in time for my uncle to get some rest and be back to work on Monday morning.

Eddie and I had never been out of Arkansas much. Once we visited my mother's sister who lived in West Plains, Missouri. The only other time we left the state was when we lived in Pocahontas, which was in a dry county. Every once in a while, my mother and stepfather would drive over the Missouri line to buy beer and whiskey. Now we were seeing many things that we had never seen before. Shortly after leaving Arkansas, we got on a four-lane Interstate highway, which amazed us, as we had never seen one before. As we would travel through large cities along the way, my aunt and uncle would try to point out sights of interest to us, but we did not seem to get too excited except when we saw a big junkyard like the one we had lived in.

We stopped that night at a large motel with a restaurant and swimming pool. After we had unloaded our luggage, we went to dinner at the beautiful restaurant. My aunt and uncle ordered the food for Eddie and me. We were not accustomed to eating in such fancy places.

When the waitress brought the bowls of salad with crackers and butter slices we thought this was our meal. Eddie made a butter sandwich with his crackers, which brought laughter from our new parents and brother. When we finished our salad and crackers, we thought dinner was over, but the waitress then returned with the largest platter of food I had ever seen. We ate until we could eat no more, which was an experience we had not had too many times in our lives.

We went back to the room and put our bathing suits on for a swim in the big pool. Things went along fine until my dinner took its toll and I tore out the seat of my swimming trunks! My aunt got me a towel and I sat out the remainder of the swimming time.

We rested well that night and early Sunday morning we were on our way again. The further north we traveled, the more snow we saw and the colder it got. In the late afternoon we arrived in Flint, Michigan, which seemed to me as big as New York City. Everywhere I looked, as we drove up I-75 through Flint Township, were stores, houses, churches, and many other buildings.

We left the expressway at Pierson Road on the west side of the city and drove just a couple miles to a beautiful subdivision. When my aunt told me we were on "our" street, my heart pounded with excitement. The street name was Greenlawn Drive. As the name implied, the lawns were green in summer and houses were beautiful. When the little white Corvair pulled into the driveway at 4301, I could not believe that this was going to be "our" house.

In reality, it was not a large house. It was a very nice house with a yard that was well kept, but to Eddie and me it was as grand as the White House in Washington, D.C. When we were shown our room, we found matching twin beds. We had never had our own beds and had always slept together, but not now! There was a beautiful bathroom with a bathtub and running water. In the backyard was a large weeping willow tree and in the summer, the most beautiful rose bushes I had ever seen. Eddie and I were overwhelmed by our new surroundings, and felt we had become rich overnight.

The neighborhood we moved into was called Manley Village and was full of kids. Many of them came to our house to see the new brothers that Donny had told everyone about. There were so many faces and names that we were unable to keep them straight for a long time.

On Monday my aunt and uncle let us take the day off from school to rest from the trip. We were glad we did not have to go to school because we did not know anyone other than neighborhood kids we had met the day before and we could not remember their names.

But early Tuesday morning, we got up and dressed for our first big day in school. Aunt Frances drove us to school, registered us, and then said goodbye. I attended the Holmes Junior High School located a little over a mile from our house. Eddie attended Selby Elementary School located just two blocks from our new home. The school I went to was a new school and much larger than I was accustomed to. About fifty percent of the students were black and I had never gone to school with black kids. In Newport the black kids had "their" own school on "their" own side of town.

I also noticed that everyone in this school talked funny, like the kids in our new neighborhood. I felt I was in a different world and I felt uncomfortable and afraid. Because of my southern drawl, my classmates would gather around me and ask me to talk. When I stared to speak, they would laugh. They were not trying to be mean, but were as fascinated with me as I was with them. They even nicknamed me Arkansas, a tag that stayed with me for years.

I thought I was getting used to moving around and meeting new circumstances, but I was beginning to feel overwhelmed by everything that was happening to me. When I got to bed that Tuesday night, I began to cry in the darkness. I did not want anyone, not even Eddie, to know I was upset, so I quietly cried myself to sleep. I missed Nanny, Julie, Newport, and even Mama. Over and over I cried to myself, "I want to go home, I want to go home." I did not know it then, but I would cry myself to sleep many times before I overcame the loneliness I was experiencing.

By the first weekend I was beginning to feel a little more at home and was so glad for the couple of days that I could get away from all the new faces. Aunt Frances had different plans. On Sunday morning, we were told to get dressed for Sunday school and church. I did not want to go to church, but when I complained my uncle gave me a stern look and told me to get ready right then. I did not argue, for I sensed that he was not as easy to push around as Mama, Nanny, and Julie. I knew I had to challenge his authority to see who was boss, but I felt this was not the time, so I just got dressed and kept quiet.

When we arrived at our new church, the worship service was just beginning. The sanctuary was almost full and Aunt Frances asked the usher to take us down the center aisle to the third pew from the front. I felt that every eye was glued on us as we walked down the long aisle and felt so relieved when we were finally in place.

I did not understand a great deal about the service, but I did find the pastor's sermon a little interesting. When the service was over adults and young people welcoming Eddie and me to the church surrounded us. When the crowd cleared Donny had to take us to meet all his friends. After meeting a host of other new faces, we were directed to our Sunday school class.

I was in the youth department with about thirty to forty other young people and only recognized a couple of faces. I felt that I had been taken to another planet and dropped off in a strange new world. I was shy and this was one of the hardest things I had ever done. I had a new home, a new family, a new school, and now church. When would it all end?

When we got home, my uncle was sitting in the living room reading the paper. He rarely went to church with us, but always made sure we did not miss a service. Aunt Frances made a good dinner for us and we gathered at the table to feast. It seems to me that we almost always had roast beef for Sunday dinner. After church on Sunday nights, I can remember eating roast beef sandwiches and watching "The F.B.I." on television.

My aunt was a wonderful cook and I learned that if I would tell her how good the desserts were, she would offer me more. I did this for a few weeks, but she caught on and would just say, "Thank you, Hal."

When we sat down to eat our meals, Aunt Frances led us in a prayer. For a long time after we moved she thanked the Lord for Eddie and me every time she prayed. We had prayed at Nanny's house, but when my aunt prayed she seemed to pray with such feeling, as though she was talking to someone who was right there listening.

When we finished eating Eddie and I helped clear the table and dry dishes. As Aunt Frances washed the dishes, she would sing one hymn after another. She did not have a professional voice, but when she sang it made me feel that God was not far away. This took place day after day as we washed the supper dishes. After a while, I began to feel very uncomfortable.

Once I was caught lying and for several nights at suppertime, Aunt Frances handed me a bible and asked me to read a verse concerning the sin of lying. Between the church services, the prayers at meals, the hymn sings over the sink, and the reading of verses, I was being saturated with my aunt's faith in God.

I watched my aunt very closely to try to find areas of inconsistency so I could discredit her testimony, but she did not seem to have any. She really meant what she was telling me, and she lived in a consistent way day by day.

There were several neighbors who had begun to attend our church because they had seen the same thing. She would take her coffee cup and go to one of the neighbor ladies' houses and while there, share with them about the church and the Lord. I saw several young couples change their styles of living because of my aunt's influence.

Reading verses from the bible was not the only form of discipline that my new foster parents used. Eddie and I lost privileges, were grounded, and received occasional spankings when we disobeyed or lied. One evening at supper, my uncle yelled at Eddie. I got mad and smarted off to him. That was the wrong thing to do. He got out of his chair, came around the table, and knocked me out of my chair. Well, this was the moment I had been waiting for and I was going to teach my uncle who was boss. We began to fight and took turns exchanging blows, but to my surprise, my uncle was not easily beaten. Mom finally got between us and stopped the two-man brawl. I never told anyone, but I was glad because I was being soundly defeated. No one told me my uncle boxed in the U.S. Army and did quite well for himself. From that time on, I thought twice before I mouthed off to him or my aunt.

I did very well in school for a while because we had already covered the material my new school was working on when I arrived. When we began to cover new material, I began to have problems. I was not used to studying and had bad behavioral problems.

I was so unsure of myself in my new surroundings that I was constantly trying to get attention or look like a tough guy. By the middle of the next marking period, I had D's in four classes and was constantly in trouble. My teachers began to make me stay after school almost every school night. I knew my aunt and uncle would not like that. One morning the principal announced that track practice would begin that week, and it was a welcome announcement. I told my aunt and uncle that I had joined the track team and would have to practice each school night, when in reality I was being punished by being kept after school. My lie continued to grow as I was asked about what events I was going out for, how many other guys were on the team, and many other things.

I kept my lie covered up until report cards were given to us to take home. I knew as soon as my aunt and uncle saw my report card, which had at least four D's on it, they would know it was all a lie. As a result of this knowledge, I kept my report card for over a week before I gave it to my aunt. I would not have given it to her then, if my teachers were not threatening to call home if I did not bring the signed report card back soon.

When I handed the card to Aunt Frances, she looked at it. Then she looked at me sternly and warned me that my uncle was not going to be happy with it. I was so used to people feeling sorry for "poor little Hal;" that her response surprised me. My uncle came home shortly thereafter and we all sat down for supper. After we prayed, Aunt Frances handed my uncle the report card. I prayed harder after she handed him the card than I did before. I had a lump in my throat so big I could not swallow water. As he stared at the card, I did not know what to expect, but I had a strong feeling this would be different from Nanny's sympathetic statements, and I was right. My uncle looked across the table at me, pointed his finger at me, and sternly warned me never to bring another report card home like this one, or I would wish I had never been born. He then laid the card aside, began to eat his supper, and never brought it up again. I got the message that day and I began to apply myself to my studies and never brought home another report like that one again. I also learned a lesson about lying. I began to realize that lying just did not pay because I always got caught.

Another problem that Eddie and I had when we arrived in Michigan was our teeth. I could only remember being in a dentist office one time. My aunt and uncle realized just by looking at our smiles that we needed to see a dentist badly. When we visited Dr. McKenzie's office the first time, he took x-rays and examined our teeth. He then reported to my aunt and uncle that we had cavities in almost every tooth in our heads. I had some teeth that were so bad they had to be pulled. My aunt and uncle paid hundreds of dollars for dental work that was the result of neglect we had experienced for years.

CHAPTER 9

Mom and Pop

Eddie and I became frustrated with the problem of what to call our aunt and uncle. We did not want to call them Aunt Frances and Uncle Donald for we wanted to feel closer to our new family than just two nephews. We also did not want to call them Daddy and Mama, for that was what we called our real parents. We thought about it and came up with the names "Mom" & "Pop." My aunt and uncle agreed to the names and from that time on, we have always referred to them in this manner. As a matter of fact, Donny started calling them Mom and Pop and does to this day.

One of the funniest things that I remember happening that first year took place in the spring. One of the guys in the neighborhood got ahold of two pairs of boxing gloves and a bunch of us organized a boxing tournament. I took on three of four of the neighborhood boys and beat them all! Pop sat on the porch patiently watching as I defeated opponent after opponent. Then when we were about finished, he stepped up and asked if he could try the gloves out. I still did not know that he had boxed in the army and I wanted another chance to teach him a lesson on manhood. As we stood eye to eye with gloves held up, he began to poke at me and after about five or six pokes to my face I got mad and swung at him wildly. Well, my swing missed, but his counter-swing did not! I found myself on the ground between the shrubs and the house. I was not going to admit defeat, so I went back into battle and soon was back in the shrubs a second time. Again I climbed from my position on the ground and attacked with wild swings and determination, but as before, I ended up back in the shrubs. When I got up the third time I was beginning to feel a little dizzy, so Pop and Eddie helped me into the house. It was after his exchange that Pop told me he had boxed in the army. As a matter of fact, he fought a "tough man" at a carnival once and defeated his opponent to win a fifty-dollar prize. Due to an injury from that fight, he had to have surgery on his arm, which cost him much more than the fifty-dollar prize money.

As summer approached, Eddie and I were more at home and I no longer cried myself to sleep. When the last report card came out for the 1963 – 64 school year, we had greatly improved in our studies. There were several reasons for this. First of all, we had someone to help us with our homework, which we both needed very badly. Also we were required to do our studies before we could go out to play ball or be involved in neighborhood activities after school. Eddie also was found by his fifth-grade teacher to have dyslexia, a learning disability that causes words to appear backwards. Once this was discovered, Eddie's school work improved one hundred percent. My studies improved so much that I got to go out for the track team, and ran in several meets before the end of the year.

Although the learning problems were much improved, I was still battling an old problem. I was still plagued with terrible nightmares that had haunted me for several years. I got to the point that I was almost afraid to go to sleep at night for fear of the nightmares. I wanted to be rid of them, but I was constantly thinking about my past with Mama. My bitterness toward her had slowly turned to hate that ate at me all the time.

I had also become keenly aware of my present spiritual condition. I knew from the sermons I was hearing, the Sunday school lessons I was being taught, and Mom's prayers that I was "lost." I was full of fear that I might die in my sleep, for I knew I would go to hell. Many nights the only way I could go to sleep was to pray the little kids' prayer: "Now I lay me down to sleep, I pray the Lord my soul to keep; if I should die before I wake, I pray the Lord my soul to take." For me, who tried to act the part of "Mr. Tough," this was not easy to do, but I could not overcome the fear in any other way.

The remainder of 1964 was a period of great adjustment, but each week we found it easier and easier. Slowly but surely we were beginning to put our past in the past, and started focusing on the future, which looked brighter than ever before.

Eddie and I were both gaining weight as a result of the good meals Mom prepared. We were continuing our weekly visits to the dentist to have our many cavities filled. Many new friendships were being formed with kids in the neighborhood and at school. We also joined Troop 256 of the Boy Scouts of America. We went on campouts, collected newspapers, and even got to usher at college football games.

There was no question that we were doing better materially, educationally, and socially. In spite of all this, we were still as spiritually lost as we were in the junkyard house or the alley apartment in Newport. Guilt still robbed me of any real joy in my life, as I still lied when I found it convenient and used profanity constantly when away from my family and teachers.

My life was also still filled with doubts about everyone around me. I did not believe that Mom and Pop really loved me, but only wanted us out of desire for money from the state. (I later dropped that idea when I found out how much they received for our care.) As a result of my suspicions, I did not tell Mom or Pop that I loved them. I never wanted to love them. I was afraid they might reject me as my mother had done.

As 1964 came to a close, it had been a hard year for Eddie and me. The difficulties, however, were so different from the year before. 1963 had many problems and almost no hope. How different now that we had a nice home, stable environment, love, and discipline!

Despite all the good things that had happened to me, I was still empty inside. In many ways I was like Absalom, King David's son. I had everything going for me, and yet kept searching for some peace, purpose, and meaning. Although I was doing everything in my power to appear tough, confident and happy, the opposite was really true. One sign of my struggle was the continuing nightmares that had plagued me for years. Night after night, week after week, I would awake trembling, sweating, sometimes crying, and always terrified. I felt as though I was some kind of prisoner trapped by those awful dreams.

Something was missing in my life and I felt I must find it, no matter what I had to do.

CHAPTER 10

A New Heart

Mom and Pop were determined to try to make up for many of the very unhappy times Eddie and I had experienced. One way they did this was by making our first Christmas with them the best we had ever known. I thought our Christmas at Nanny's was great, but the Christmas Mom and Pop gave us was even bigger. There were so many presents under the beautiful Christmas tree that we had no room for scrap paper and boxes. We would have to clear the floor then open more presents! It was a good Christmas. Eddie and I were so excited and thankful for a real family.

After opening presents we sat in the living room and sang Christmas songs. Pop played Daddy's guitar, which had been in his possession for many years. We got out the reel-to-reel tape recorder and made a tape of our first Christmas. When we listen to that tape now, we all laugh together, for Eddie and I couldn't carry a tune in a bucket. Mom fixed a beautiful Christmas dinner, which was the icing on the cake of a great Christmas Day.

Although the presents, fun, and food were swell, I still ached with emptiness. I kept wondering how I could have so much and yet still be so lonely and sad inside. It just did not make any sense to me. Nothing seemed to meet the need I had to sense wholeness. I did not know then, but it would not be long until I would find what I longed for. I would have my own "Christmas Day" that would overshadow all other Christmases.

As the new year started there was a lot of excitement around our church. The pastor announced the first Sunday of January that we were having revival services. The services were to begin the last Sunday of January and close the first Sunday in February. I was not even sure what revival services were, but I did know I got enough church on Sundays and Wednesdays. I sure did not want to attend church services every night for a week.

When we got to Sunday school that morning, which followed the worship service, it was announced that there was going to be a contest. The entire youth department was divided into two teams. The contest was to see which could have the most young people, regulars, and visitors attending the revival services. When I saw the team I was on and heard the foe's threats of defeat, I decided that maybe I could attend one or two of the services.

By the last Sunday in January both teams were working to win the contest. I could not figure out why people got so excited about revival services. What could be that exciting about sitting and listening to someone preach or sing?

My best friend at church was a boy named Joe Hill. Joe's parents were Christians, but Joe, like me, only attended church and Sunday school under pressure. Joe and I had sat in the parking lot many times in his parents' car during Sunday evening services. His parents told him that he had to go to each revival service, and he begged me to come so he would not have to endure it alone. I reluctantly agreed to try to be there each night, even though it was the last thing I really wanted to do.

The first Sunday of revival services Bethlehem United Methodist Church was quite full. As we sat in our regular pew, third from the front on the right side, I waited to see the evangelist. I did not recall seeing an evangelist before and I wondered what such a person looked like. When the pastor came on to the platform, two men and a woman accompanied him. One of the men appeared very old with almost no hair on his head. I thought that this man could not possibly be the evangelist. He looked too old to walk, much less preach. Pastor Hastings introduced the trio. I was taken aback, for the old man was the evangelist. His name was Dr. J.C. McPheeters. The other man and woman were introduced as the song evangelists, Charles and Janet Shepherd.

The service that Sunday morning included the Shepherds singing some songs and a message by Dr. McPheeters. I expected a boring sermon from an old man who needed to be in a nursing home, not preaching a revival, but was I wrong! This old man was more exciting than anyone I had ever seen or heard before. He preached loud, clapped his hands, shouted, and even jumped in the air once. I had never seen anything like this before and I was glued to his every move throughout the entire sermon. When he finished his sermon, he asked for people to come forward to receive Jesus as their Savior. A host of people from all over the church stepped into the aisles, and walked forward, and knelt at the altars. I had seen a few people kneel at the altar from time to time in my year at the church, but nothing like this.

That night our youth contest began, and almost every young person from our department was there. Joe and I stayed until the team count was taken, then we slipped out to his parents' car to listen to the radio. Toward the end of the service, we sneaked back into our back row seats so our parents would not miss us when the service was over. This was only possible because I was not required to sit with Mom on Sunday nights as I was for Sunday morning worship.

When we got settled back into our seats, the preacher was still preaching. I sat and listened, for he seemed to have something about him that held my attention like no other speaker I had ever heard. When he finished he invited seekers to come to pray at the altar. Several people, including some of my friends from Sunday school, responded to his invitation. Joe and I just stood staring at the floor as others made their way to the front, where the pastor and the evangelist waited for them. When the invitation was over, we got out of the church as quickly as possible. I felt very uneasy and even felt like I wanted to go and pray, but that was not for a tough guy like me. I would never do that.

When I got home, we ate roast beef sandwiches and watched "The F.B.I." on TV. I was hoping that would get my mind off the service and the strange way I felt during the invitation. Soon it was time for bed and I knew there was a good chance that another night of nightmares would soon be mine.

As I lay in bed, I kept hearing the preacher in my mind. Over and over he kept saying, "God loves you, God loves you, God loves you." I could not get to sleep until I prayed my "Now I lay me down to sleep..." prayer, for my fear of death became so real, I almost trembled. That night the nightmares did come and I woke breathing heavily, as if someone were choking me. As I lay in the quietness I could hear my heart racing. It seemed as if it would jump from my chest. After a while, I calmed down and my mind again went back to the preacher saying, "God loves you, God loves you." I could not understand why I kept thinking about something I wanted nothing to do with. It seemed I could not get away from it.

The next night Joe and I once again sneaked from the church after the team counts to sit in the parking lot. When the service was almost over, we quietly re-entered the sanctuary. Something strange was coming over me, for that night I wanted to go back into the service a little earlier. I wanted to hear what the preacher had to say. Joe was surprised when I insisted that we get back in early. He did not want to sit in the car alone, so he went with me.

Each night we spent less time in the car and more time listening to Dr. McPheeters. By the next Sunday we were staying in the service from beginning to end. It seemed incredible that I would voluntarily go to a church service and listen to someone preach. I had fought church attendance by coming up with any excuse I could think of to keep from going. Now I was almost excited about getting there! I thought maybe it was the contest or maybe the girls were catching my attention. These were important, but it was more.

I did not understand then, but the Holy Spirit was drawing me and calling me to make a decision to follow Christ. Mom's prayers and the seed of the Word of God that had been planted over the previous few years were beginning to bear fruit. The little bible I received at school, the sermon on hell I laughed at, Uncle George's funeral, the Baptist church in Newport, and the sermons and Sunday school lessons at Bethlehem were all bringing conviction to my heart.

On Sunday night, February 6, 1965, the closing service of the revival was held. Joe and I sat in the next to last pew on the left side of the church. We would have sat in the last pew, but it was full when we got to it. As Pastor Hastings introduced the Shepherds for the last time, I felt sad. For some unknown reason I did not want the services to end. There had been such a warm feeling of love and caring in the church all week. I wanted it to go on.

Following Dr. McPheeters' introduction and his words of appreciation and farewell, the preacher began his message. This old man preached, as I had never seen anybody preach. He poured out his heart to us to respond to God's love. As he preached I could sense my heart beating faster and faster as I realized that I wanted to go to the altar. I became more and more convinced that this was what I was searching for. I needed Christ, but I could not walk to an altar in front of all the people, especially my cohort in crime, my brother Eddie.

As Dr. McPheeters closed his message, he opened the altar for those who wished to pray. We all stood as Mr. and Mrs. Shepherd sang a song. People from all over the sanctuary crowded the altars. I wanted to step out, but I just could not seem to humble myself to do it. As I saw others crying, hugging, and lifting their hands in praise, I yearned to be with them.

Finally, the singing stopped and the congregation was seated. My heart sank as I realized that what I yearned for was at my fingertips and slipping away. Then the pastor asked for some people to come and pray for those seeking help. I decided that I would go and pretend to pray for others, but in reality pray for myself. Joe looked puzzled as I stepped out to go pray for others when he knew I was as lost as he was.

When I got to the front of the church, I knelt behind one of the kids in the youth group and bowed my head. I did not know how to pray but my heart cried to God to forgive me and give me meaning and purpose. When my friend returned to her seat, I moved forward and knelt at the altar to pray. As I prayed, the tears began to flow from my eyes. I began to ask God to forgive all my sins. As I prayed, something marvelous happened. I felt as though a heavy weight was being lifted off my shoulders. I also felt as though God reached down and put His arms of love and forgiveness around me and just held me. I had never experienced such a feeling of love, forgiveness, and being clean. All I could pray was "God forgive me, God forgive me." I felt so bad that I had hurt God so many times when he loved me so much. I was at the altar for what seemed a long time I just cried and kept asking over and over for God to forgive me.

As the other seekers left the altar, I found myself alone. Our pastor and Dr. McPheeters came and talked to me and prayed for me. After we were finished praying, I went to my friend Joe to tell him what had happened to me. When I got back to our pew, I found Joe kneeling, crying, and praying with his mother and sister. I got as close to him as possible and I said, "Joe, we are in the same boat and it's sinking fast. I'm getting off while I can."

I arose from the pew and started for the door. I wanted to get home to tell Mom what had happened. She had not been in the service and I wanted her to pray with me. I also wanted to tell her how much I loved her.

As I was leaving the sanctuary, an elderly man stopped me. He looked at me and said, "How are things with your soul, Brother Phillips?" For the first time in my life I could honestly say everything was all right. I hugged Mr. Branstner and told him how Jesus had helped me. Then I headed for home to tell Mom the good news of my salvation.

I ran from the church, across the front lawn, across Clio Road, a busy four-lane highway, and into Manley Village. I jumped two fences and ran down Greenlawn Drive to our home. When I entered the back door, I slammed the door, so everyone would know that I was home. I then went immediately to my bedroom, where I fell on my knees beside the bed. As I wept and prayed, Pop came into the room and asked what was wrong. I told him I had given my heart to Jesus. He just turned and left the room with a puzzled look on his face.

A few minutes later, Mom came into the room and also asked what was wrong. I told her that I had given my heart to Jesus and asked her to pray for me. Mom knelt down beside me and put her arms around me and prayed a beautiful prayer. I cried like a baby as she held me in her arms.

When she finished praying, I told her for the first time how much I loved her and thanked her for her prayers.

Following our prayer time together, I changed clothes and got in bed. As I lay in the darkness, the tears continued to flow. I prayed over and over, "Please forgive me, Lord, please forgive me, Lord," until I fell asleep. That night I slept better than any night I could remember. There was no fear of death and no nightmares. As a matter of fact, the nightmares stopped and never returned. I had never felt as safe and peaceful as I did the night of February 6th.

The next morning I awakened to a new day as well as a new life. I could not wait to tell my neighborhood friends what had happened to me. As I ran from the house to meet Dan and Daryl, two of my classmates, I noticed that everything seemed different. The sky appeared bluer, the snow appeared whiter, and the air seemed to smell so fresh and clean. It was as though the whole world had changed. In reality, it was the same and it was I who had changed! I was a new person, just as II Corinthians 5:17 states, "Therefore if any man be in Christ He is a new creature: Old things are passed away; behold all things are become new." (KJV)

Praise be to God for His wonderful power to save, to forgive, to cleanse, to give purpose and meaning to life. David expressed it well when he said, "Blessed is he whose transgression is forgiven, whose sins are covered. Blessed is the man whose sin the Lord does not count against him and in whose spirit is no deceit." Psalm 32:1-2 (NIV)

CHAPTER 11

The Road to Revival

The months that followed my conversion were the most exciting months I had ever lived. I wanted everyone to know that Jesus had become my Savior. I witnessed to my friends, neighbors, teachers, and anyone else who would listen. My methods were not always the best, and I had to learn to allow the Holy Spirit to work rather than trying to witness in my own strength. Although there was much rejection from those I witnessed to, God's Word burned in my heart and I felt I had to tell of His love.

A few months after my salvation, I was asked to speak to our church youth group. I had never spoken in front of a group before and I was very nervous. As I stood to share the message, I would check the ideas off in my notes. When I got about halfway through the message, I began to get excited and started speaking louder and waving my arms. I made a sweeping motion with my right arm and the pencil I was holding flew from my hand. It sailed over the heads of my listeners and bounced off the wall behind them! I was embarrassed as everyone laughed, but I soon regained my composure and finished the message.

As we were leaving the youth room, Mrs. Hastings, our pastor's wife and youth leader asked if she could have a word with me. My first thought was that I had really messed up and she was going to correct me. Instead the kind lady complimented me on my message and told me that she thought God was calling me to preach. I was so excited about what she had said that I could not wait to get home to tell my family.

When I arrived home, I announced to Mom, Pop, Eddie, and Donny that Mrs. Hastings thought I was called to preach. Pop said, "Well, that's just what we need around here, a preacher." He then chuckled and Eddie and Donny joined in the laughter. Then Mom got out of her chair, and with tears in her eyes, she walked toward me, put her arms around me, and told me how proud she would be to have a son who was a preacher.

I was so happy about what God was doing for me, but I felt a deep burden for my brother. He was just not interested in knowing my Jesus, but I prayed for him every day. I was like Andrew who wanted so for his brother Peter to come to meet Jesus. Little did I know then that like Peter, my brother Eddie would someday be a preacher of The Gospel.

In May of 1966, Dr. Ford Philpot held an evangelistic crusade at the I.M.A. (Industrial Mutual Association) Auditorium in Downtown Flint. I had been praying for my brother for over a year and was hoping with all my heart that he would soon become a Christian. One night during the crusade, Eddie stepped into the aisle and walked to the front of the huge auditorium to give his heart to Christ.

As I went forward to stand by my brother, my heart leaped for joy within me and I wanted to shout, "Praise God!" We went to a counseling room where we prayed together for the first time as spiritual brothers as well as physical brothers.

Within a few years Eddie experienced the call of God upon his life to preach The Gospel. At first preaching did not come as easy to Eddie as it did for me. His first few attempts at preaching were disastrous. Mom and Pop tried to persuade him that he must have been mistaken, but Eddie kept preaching anytime he got the chance.

It was not until my senior year that I surrendered to God's call to preach. I had had my ups and downs spiritually through high school. Now I had to look seriously at my future, for I was only a few months from graduation.

One Sunday morning our new pastor, Reverend Cookingham, introduced Reverend Rudd, who was to sing in the service. Brother Bill, as I learned to call him, was to serve our church as a missionary intern for the next nine months. Brother Bill shared his testimony in the service and then he sang a beautiful song. As I listened to the words of "Ten Thousand Angels" my heart was deeply touched. I bowed my head and asked the Lord to take me completely and use me for his glory. I surrendered to preach wherever he would want me to share His "Good News" with others. From that day I have sought God's will for my life and determined to obey his direction. In the months that followed I had many opportunities to preach in churches, rescue missions, nursing homes, and even on street corners. The greatest joy of my life had become serving Jesus, and my favorite activity was preaching.

My first experience of preaching in a regular church service took place during my senior year. Reverend Rudd contacted a pastor friend in Flint that he had gone to seminary with. The two ministers decided to schedule a special youth service on a Sunday evening.

Our youth group was buzzing with excitement, as we were told our youth choir would be singing and I would be preaching. We started practicing our choir number and I began to prepare my first official sermon. I was anxious for the date of the service to arrive, but the closer it got, the more nervous I became.

Finally, the weekend of our big engagement arrived. The youth choir had their last rehearsals and I put the final touches on my message. When we arrived at the church and entered the sanctuary, I was taken aback. It was the longest sanctuary I had ever seen. From the back row the pulpit looked so small. I wondered if people sitting there could even see the preacher. We went to the choir loft, practiced our songs once more and waited for the "crowds" to arrive.

When it was time to begin the service, the "crowds" had still not arrived, but there were about twenty-five teenagers present. They filled the last three rows of the long sanctuary and appeared miles from the platform. Our choir sang and gave testimonies before I was introduced to speak.

As I stood, I could see the pastor of the church sitting near the front of the sanctuary. He appeared a little nervous as this "rookie" preacher stepped behind his pulpit. I preached my heart out to the young people and then gave an invitation to make a full commitment to Christ.

The youth choir sang two or three verses of an invitation song while I stood praying with my eyes closed. When I looked up, expecting that someone had responded and come to pray, I noticed that no one had moved. I asked the choir to stop singing and I "dared" the teenagers to have enough "guts" to serve Jesus. I told them they were chickens if they let their friends keep them from following Jesus.

As I gave this unsophisticated challenge, the pastor got up and walked out of the service. He was upset that I had come on so strong and went to his office in protest of my methods.

I asked the choir to sing another verse. As they began to sing, the entire group of young people walked together from the back of the sanctuary! There was tremendous rejoicing as these young men and women prayed through to victory. Several of the teens gave testimonies, asked for forgiveness, and gave hugs.

Reverend Rudd went to the pastor's study to tell him of the good news. When he arrived, he found the pastor to be very upset. He began to lecture our leader about how it was "out of place" for me to preach as I did. When he finished his lecture, Reverend Rudd asked him to come to the sanctuary. Upon entering and seeing the teens of his church singing and praising God around the altar, a shocked look came across his face. He had been praying for this breakthrough, but did not expect it at this service.

The pastor later asked for forgiveness and confessed that his preaching had been too "easy." He committed himself that night to give a greater challenge, his church began to grow until the long sanctuary could no longer hold the crowds, and a much larger sanctuary had to be built. He still served as pastor of this large and growing congregation, almost twenty years later.

This wonderful service was truly the work of the Holy Spirit, but I decided that I had much to do with it! My pride began to grow and soon I was taking credit for what had taken place. Proverbs 16:18 tells us, "Pride goes before destruction, a haughty spirit before a fall." (NIV) That's exactly what happened to me.

When Pastor Cookingham heard of the wonderful service, he asked our youth group to take charge of the Sunday evening service the next week. I was excited about this opportunity to "impress" the people in my home church. Little did I know that this would become one of the most humbling nights of my life.

As the service began that Sunday night, I felt confident and self-reliant. The youth choir sang beautifully and gave several moving testimonies. Everything went well until I stood and tried to preach. I could not understand what was happening as I became lost in my notes and thoughts. The harder I tried, the more confused the congregation and I became. Finally, I finished the sermon and walked from the platform.

Normally the speaker went to the back of the sanctuary to shake hands. I was so embarrassed, I went to the pastor's study, fell on my knees and wept like a baby. I could not face the people. Pastor Cookingham came into the office shortly after I arrived and knelt beside me. He assured me that this was a good learning experience and in the future, I would praise the Lord for teaching me a special lesson.

Now I look back on that night and I am so thankful for the important truth that I learned. Many times I have thought of that night. It is a constant reminder that "through Christ I can do all things" (Philippians 4:13) and without Him I can do nothing.

Although I was doing my best to serve the Lord, I was still a teenager and full of mischief. I used to enjoy pulling harmless pranks on Mom. One night I took a small squirt bottle filled with warm water to the dinner table. Our dog Fleagle was always sitting under the table, waiting for a scrap of food. As we sat eating, I leaned under the table and squirted some of the warm water on Mom's leg and exclaimed, "Fleagle, what are you doing?" Mom jumped to her feet convinced that Fleagle had wet on her leg! Everyone except Mom laughed when I held up the small bottle of water. After she calmed down a little, she laughed too.

Another teenage activity that I was very involved in was talking on the telephone. Mom constantly had to get after me for talking too long, especially to my girlfriends. The problem worsened, because of the telephone extension in the basement family room. One day I called Pastor Cookingham from the basement to ask about a church activity. In the middle of our conversation, Mom picked up the phone in the kitchen and began to chew me out. She was sure I was talking to my girlfriend as she began to give a lecture to our pastor about talking too long on the phone. She then ordered me to come for dinner and hung up. I apologized to Reverend Cookingham and went to eat. After Mom prayed, she looked sternly at me and asked who I was talking to on the phone. When I told her it was the pastor, a shocked look came across her face. She did not know whether to believe me or not until Reverend Cookingham came to the front door. I let him in, and we stood and laughed together. When Mom saw that the pastor was not offended, she laughed with us. After that Mom always asked who I was speaking to before giving me a lecture.

After high school graduation, I attended Asbury College, where I was a freshman during the Great 1970 Asbury Revival. This revival was the most marvelous moving of God's presence I have ever seen. For eight days and nights we experienced the presence of the Holy Spirit in a way that completely transformed our campus.

Following the revival, requests began to flood into the college office for witness teams to come to churches to tell of the revival. I soon found myself in a different church every weekend, sharing the wonderful works of God. Our teams traveled all over the Midwest and God brought revival to church after church.

I was asked one weekend to travel with a witness team to Anderson, Indiana. Anderson is the home of Anderson College and the world headquarters of the Church of God. Our team was asked to share in services Saturday night, Sunday morning and Sunday night at the South Meridian Church of God.

On Sunday evening revival broke out in the church and soon spread to the nearby college. Our witness team returned to Asbury on Monday, but services continued for fifty days as the revival spread. It was estimated that 5,000 people were converted to Christ during the Anderson Revival.

During spring quarter at Asbury, God began to speak to me about leading a crusade in Flint, the city I called home. As the Lord spoke to me,

I wrote down dates, places, and names, as they would come to my mind. I prayed for weeks about this matter and became convinced that this was God's will.

When I arrived home in June, I announced to my family that I was not going to get a summer job, but was going to lead a citywide crusade. Mom and Pop were not very happy, for they felt I needed a job to raise money for my sophomore year at Asbury.

I contacted a Christian friend by the name of John Matthews to work with me. John and I had graduated from high school together and were good friends. John agreed to help me with the crusade and we began to contact churches. We wrote to over 300 churches, asking for permission to come and share about the Asbury Revival. Slowly but surely speaking engagements began to come in and we were on our way!

John and I reserved the 5,000-seat I.M.A. Auditorium, where Eddie was saved, for ten days. The rental fee alone was $5,000. We believed God would provide the money.

During the following weeks we saw one miracle after another take place. Revival broke out in several churches as we shared how God was working. More and more pastors and people became excited about the crusade and began working with us.

One of the churches I wrote to ask permission to speak was the Bethel Park Free Methodist Church. The pastor later told me that when he received my letter, he read it and threw it in the wastepaper basket. The Lord then directed him to remove the letter from the trash and call me. On July 19th I arrived at the church to speak in the evening service. As my custom was, I read several newspaper articles about the Asbury Revival, shared some of my experiences, and gave a challenge to the people. I told them that they too could have a great revival if they would just obey God completely. When we began to sing an invitation song, God moved mightily upon the congregation. Over half the people moved out to surrender themselves to the Lord. After a long period of prayer around the altars, people started sharing what God had done for them. After several testimonies, singing would break out and more people would make their way to the altar to surrender to Jesus. The excitement in the service was so intense that a lady had a heart attack and paramedics had to come assist her. The congregation moved into the fellowship hall and the service continued. The lady later had a full recovery, but we knew she would never forget that service.

The revival at Bethel Park lasted almost a year. Pastor Vibbert reported to me that many Sundays he never preached as the Holy Spirit moved. Testimonies were given and people responded to the call of Christ. The people of the church also became very involved in our crusade effort. Of all the churches I spoke to that summer, they became our leading supporter.

One afternoon I received a phone call from an elderly gentleman in the Flint area. He wanted to meet with me concerning the crusade. I made an appointment with him and when we met, he told me God had instructed him to give me some money. This was definitely an answer to prayer, for we needed the rent money for the auditorium almost immediately. After talking for a while, he handed me a check for $8,000! Later he came to me and gave me another check for $3,000. We paid the rent on the auditorium and used the remainder of the funds to advertise the crusade. We bought full-page ads in the *Flint Journal*, printed and distributed over 50,000 flyers, and bought prime-time spots on two television stations.

The crusade was to begin on Saturday, August 15th, with a "March for Christ" through downtown Flint. We obtained a permit from the City Council and warned the police to be prepared for a large crowd. The police were skeptical, but when the march began an estimated 5,000 brothers and sisters in Christ marched from the I.M.A. parking lot shouting, "Jesus is Lord!"

For ten days thousands of people attended the "New Life Crusade" and hundreds of people came to know Jesus as Savior. Some felt the crusade would not succeed because we had no big-name preacher. As a matter of fact, we had no preacher at all. The services were giant testimony services similar to the services at Asbury and Anderson. Some nights there would be four or five invitations during the service, with dozens of people responding each time. It was a wonderful experience to see God moving on the people of my hometown.

When the crusade ended at the I.M.A., we were persuaded to move to the West Court Street Church of God. At this beautiful church the crusade continued for another seven days. As at the I.M.A., many more people accepted Christ, as all present sensed the moving of God in each service.

The last night of the crusade the congregation took up a special offering for John and me. Our song leader came up with the idea and announced the special offering without even asking us. Our method of taking offerings was to have the ushers stand at the doors at the close of each service. Those wishing to give just dropped their gift in the offering buckets. When the money was counted and divided evenly, I found I had more money to return to college than the year before after working all summer in a General Motors factory.

It was only days after the close of the New Life Crusade that I packed my bags and headed back to school. I was eager to share with my classmates what God had done in Flint. As I began to share my experiences, I found that many other students had similar scenes in their homes across the Midwest. Truly it was a summer of miracles in many towns and cities.

I returned to Flint in the summer of 1971 in hopes of repeating the crusade of 1970. Although we worked as hard as before and prayed much, it did not seem to be God's will to work as He had the previous summer. We did have a "March for Christ" and a crusade, but everything was on a much more abbreviated scale.

In June I was approached by the Bethel Park Free Methodist Church about the possibility of serving as an evangelist for a crusade. This crusade was very different from what I had been used to. The church youth group had been invited to travel to Epworth, Georgia to hold a week of Bible School in the local Free Methodist Church. It was decided that evening services should also be held, thus the need for an evangelist. After praying about it I agreed to go, but wondered to myself what I was getting into.

When we arrived at the church after driving for most of two days, we were shocked at the sight we beheld. The church building was a small block structure that had never been painted inside or out. The grass was knee deep and there was not a sign identifying it as a church. The church had no pastor and the record attendance was six. I could not figure out why God had led me to this place when I had so much to do back in Flint. I felt like Phillip when he was called to go to the desert.

We began to work and plan immediately. The grass was mowed, the building swept and mopped. The interior and exterior were painted and teams went out to find Bible School prospects. All this was accomplished in the midst of very uncooperative weather. It rained at least once a day every day for almost two weeks.

In just a few days the building was ready for Bible School to begin. The team gathered children from around the community and the morning sessions were under way. The children expressed excitement over what we were doing, but I knew there must be more God wanted to accomplish.

That night we had our first preaching service. The only people present were the twenty-five or so people from the community, yet I did not know how to get them there. After a good time of prayer at the close of the service, several of the young people decided to go into town.

Earlier in the afternoon we had been at a local grocery store, where we met a young man named Danny. I asked Danny where the local teenagers hung out. He gave me directions to a shopping center about five miles from the church. Several of us decided that we were going witnessing at that shopping center after church.

When we arrived at our destination we found that Danny was right. There were scores of young people scattered around the parking lot of the small shopping center. We broke into groups and went to get acquainted. The teenagers were friendly and very responsive, especially the fellows who took a special liking to several of the girls in our group.

The group I was in moved into a crowd of youth and invited them to our services. While we were talking, a local policeman drove into the parking lot. He got out of his car, walked over to me and began to accuse me of trying to corrupt "his young people." I denied his accusation and told him I was there to share my faith in Christ. He pointed down toward my feet and asked what I was drinking. When I looked down, I found that next to my food was an empty beer bottle. I told him it was not mine, but he ordered me to get my gang together and get out of the parking lot or he was taking me to jail. I could not believe what was happening, but I called for everyone to load up and head back to the church.

When we arrived back at the church, we found that two carloads of the teenagers had followed us. We stood around for quite a while, visiting with them and sharing the gospel. That night a young man named Dash Tally gave his heart to the Lord and God began to move in Epworth, Georgia.

Two days after Dash's conversion he preached in the evening service. The church was full of his friends who had come to see what had happened to their friend. At the close of the service Dash gave an invitation and several of his friends, gave their hearts to the Savior. It was a glorious sight to see Dash praying with his friends as they found their way to salvation. These new Christians in turn invited other friends to the little church and the scene was repeated night after night.

When our scheduled two-week stay in Epworth had come to an end, it was decided that four of us would stay and continue the revival services. The remainder of the crusade team headed back to Michigan, but God continued to move as dozens of young people from all over the area came to the services to accept Christ. The little church was full to capacity night after night. One night the crowd was so large that some people had to stand outside, watching and listening through the windows.

When the third week came to a close, we counted over 100 young people who had received Christ and His gift of eternal life. Many of them are today actively serving God and some, including Dash Tally, are in full-time Christian service. While driving back to Michigan, our hearts and minds overflowed with praise for the miracle God had performed at the little Free Methodist Church in Epworth, Georgia.

One of the members of the Epworth Church was Miss Laura Waters. She always referred to me as her little brother in Jesus. Many times,

Miss Laura would write to me and send me a check to help with college expenses. The wonderful thing was that without telling her, she would always send a check for the exact amount I was praying for. She truly knew the voice of the Holy Spirit and she was obedient.

During January of 1972, another incident took place that showed me very clearly that God had a purpose in life for me. My car had broken down in Northern Ohio, and for several weeks a classmate named Ed Cain, traveled with me to my weekend revivals. Ed had a red Ford Mustang and volunteered to provide transportation to my speaking engagements. Ed and I had traveled with a four-man gospel team we called "God's Squad" following the Asbury Revival. We had some great times and now we were hitting the road again. Little did I know then that we were going to hit more than the road!

One weekend Ed and I were invited to a small Wesleyan Church in Miamisburg, Ohio. Miamisburg is located just south of Dayton, Ohio, and about two hours from Asbury. We had a great weekend at the church as the Holy Spirit touched many lives and victories were won.

We finished our special services on Sunday evening and after a good night's rest, we headed back to Kentucky. It was a bright sunny day and the air was cold and crisp. The night before, three or four inches of snow had fallen, but we found the roads in pretty good condition. As we pulled onto I-75, the expressway was in good shape and we traveled at the posted seventy-mile-per-hour speed without any problem. At least for a little while there were no problems.

We crossed the Ohio River into Covington, Kentucky, and decided to stop for a pop. We exited the expressway and found a store with a soda fountain. Ed and I both got a large cup of Coke before continuing our journey home.

We had not traveled long until we came to the top of a hill. Our car was in the left lane of three lanes of traffic when we topped the hill. Things were going fine until we came upon an awful sight. The right two lanes of the expressway were only wet, but our lane was covered with deep slush. Apparently a snowplow had plowed all the slush and snow into our lane. As a result, we were in trouble.

When the little red car hit the deep slush it began to fish tail violently. Ed did all he could to get the car straightened out, but it seemed to be no use. We went into a spin at seventy miles per hour and I knew only the Lord could help us. The car did several 360° turns as Ed and I sat totally helpless. Ed turned to me during those moments and said, "Hal, the Lord is with us!" I responded with assurance of His presence.

On one of the spins, I looked north and was terrified to see a semi-tractor trailer coming south in the right lane. As I saw his direction and speed, it dawned on me that were going to collide. We spun into the right lane just as the huge truck was passing at sixty-five miles per hour!

Something happened during those moments that I have never been able to explain, except to say it was a miracle. As the truck came racing toward our little car, I shouted to Ed, "The truck is going to hit us!" As soon as I got the words out of my mouth, everything seemed to suddenly move in slow motion. The tractor passed by, but our car slid under the trailer. The rear wheels hit the side of our car. Instead of the terrible crushing that I expected, it was as though we had only been bumped very softly.

In just a few seconds we were spinning in the opposite direction and events returned to normal speed. The car continued to spin until we were back in the left lane. The car stopped spinning and Ed drove the car into the median. As we came to a stop, I looked down at the cup of Coke I held in my hand. A semi-truck traveling sixty-five miles per hour had just hit us and not a drop of my pop had spilled. Ed and I had experienced a miracle! When the car came to a stop, we jumped from the car and began to praise God for saving our lives.

The truck driver stopped his truck and ran back to where we were. He excitedly told us what had happened from his perspective. He was positive that our car was going under the trailer, but at the last moment everything changed. He told us that it was as if a "big hand" had reached under his truck and pulled our car from beneath the crushing rear wheels. We told him that the big hand he was talking about was our God and that he had saved our lives.

In a few minutes a Kentucky State Trooper arrived on the scene to get an accident report. After gathering all the facts, he informed us that he had never investigated an accident like ours where someone was not killed. He described how the truck should have run over our car, crushing us to death. Well, after hearing this, Ed and I did a little more praising the Lord!

The left side of the car was heavily damaged, but we were able to drive it. We drove to the bottom of the hill to the Florence, Kentucky, exit. There we stopped and ate supper. Ed also called his parents in Pennsylvania to tell them of our miracle. We had a chicken and dumpling supper and we headed home once again. Later that evening, I lifted in a weightlifting tournament at the college. The trophy I won that night is a constant reminder of God's protection for two of His children.

The summer of 1972, the Free Methodist Church in Savannah, Georgia invited me to bring a team for a two-week revival. I decided to ask Dash Tally, Kent Olney, who was on our Epworth team, and my brother Eddie to share the preaching responsibilities. A trio of girls from Asbury known as the Gospelites joined us to provide the special music. Each evening the girls sang and Dash, Kent, Eddie or I would preach.

This was Eddie's first experience of preaching in a revival and he was very nervous. He chose to be last on the schedule, so he had a few days to work on his sermon. When the fourth service came around Eddie was confident he had his message all set. I sat in the front row to give all the support I could to the pulpit rookie, and he needed it! Eddie got about halfway through his sermon on "Jonah and the Whale" when he seemed to lose his train of thought. He stood silent for a few moments just staring down at the pulpit, then he looked at me and asked me to come and finish the sermon. He later told me that he preached Jonah into the belly of the whale, but could not remember how to get him out.

Eddie was discouraged, but during the next few days, we helped him with his preparation for his second sermon. When he preached it, he made it all the way through! The Lord blessed the message and several people received definite help. Eddie had preached his first "complete" revival sermon, but I knew it would not be his last.

Following the services in Savannah, I was eager to get back to Flint to share with my family and church how God had blessed the first revival Eddie and I had preached together.

In the fall, I returned to Asbury College as a senior. It was wonderful to see my classmates and to share with them the blessings of the summer. Another thing that made my return to Asbury very special was that Eddie was entering Asbury as a freshman. That was a good year, as Eddie and I had opportunities to travel to many churches, where we would preach and sing together. I had mixed emotions as graduation came. I was glad to be finished with college, but sad to see the Phillips brothers team break up.

Eddie got very sick, lovesick, and returned to Michigan to be near his future wife. He finished college at John Wesley College in Owosso, Michigan. He and Karen Walker were married in 1974.

Following Eddie's college graduation, he became the pastor of the Bangor Baptist Church, near Bay City, Michigan. That year the church was the fastest growing Southern Baptist Church in Michigan. After pastoring for eight years in the Baptist and Free Methodist churches, Eddie was appointed as general evangelist to the Free Methodist Church and has served as an evangelist for over 25 years.

Chapter 12

Lexington

Since the day I surrendered to God to preach the Gospel in the fall of 1968, I had never seriously considered being a pastor. I had always believed that God had called me to be an evangelist and I had enjoyed that ministry during my years at Asbury College. As I came to the end of my college years, I began praying for God's plan for my future ministry. I was sure that I would continue to be an evangelist preaching revivals across the country. I soon found out that God had other plans.

I was now married and had submitted an application to attend Asbury Theological Seminary. I was so certain that I would be attending Asbury Seminary. I purchased a mobile home in a trailer park owned by the seminary. I found out in early summer that I had been accepted as a seminary student and planned to begin my studies at Asbury Seminary in September of 1973.

During the summer of 1973, I continued to preach at several camps and churches when something happened that I never expected. The invitations to preach at churches and camps suddenly stopped coming. I thought it was a temporary pause in my evangelistic ministry and the invitations would soon resume. As time went on I realized I was wrong.

I traveled to my last scheduled camp in August of 1973, and I questioned God about what was happening. I would soon find out that God had other plans for me and those plans changed the course of my life.

At the summer youth camp in Tennessee, I was approached by the Conference Superintendent who told me he had a church in Lexington, Kentucky for me to pastor. I was taken aback by his offer and assured him

I was an evangelist and had no intention of ever pastoring a church. He asked me to pray about it and let him know if I was interested.

As much as I tried, I could not get away from that conversation. I did begin to pray and I soon discovered that God WAS leading me to be the pastor of the Church in Lexington. This appointment seemed perfect as the church had a parsonage in which to live, they paid $85 a week and was not too far from Asbury Seminary. I could still attend seminary and pastor the church part time.

After I had agreed to accept the appointment and met with the church board, I was informed by the Conference Superintendent that the church would not accept a seminary student to be their pastor. For them to accept me as the new pastor of this church, I had to give up my plans to attend seminary. I was very surprised but as I prayed, I felt strongly that God was leading me to be their pastor and in mid-August, I received word of my official appointment effective September 1, 1973.

I was very excited but I had a problem. It was still 2 weeks before I would begin my new ministry and I had no income during those two weeks as I had no revivals scheduled. I earnestly prayed that God would open a door for me to provide some income during those two weeks.

My wife was working at the University of Kentucky Medical Center in the x-ray department. She came home the day after I cried out to God for a "two week job" to tell me of a job opening to fill in for a transporter who was going on a two week vacation. Once again God had answered my prayers and I was praising His Holy Name.

When I started my pastorate in September of 1973, I was very "cocky" as a young 23 year old pastor. I had had much success as an evangelist and had seen God bring mighty revival in many places but somewhere along the way I began to think it was because of me. I needed to be humbled and God knew where to send me for that humbling.

On my very first Sunday as "Pastor Hal," I was approached by a man following the sermon who asked if he could speak to me in private. We went to the Sunday School office downstairs where the man informed that "I had stolen the church from him." He felt strongly that he should have been the pastor and I was responsible for that not happening. He was a senior at Asbury Seminary and an ordained elder. He stated that he had more education, more experience and was by far the better choice to pastor the church. He then promised me that he would do everything possible to make my life miserable until I left so he could take over. I will say this about him. He kept his promise and made the next year one of the most difficult periods of time in my entire 40 years of ministry.

As excited as I was when I began my ministry as a pastor, my years at the church in Lexington were very hard. I soon came to find out that the leadership of the church wanted to sell the church and parsonage, which was located on the north end of Lexington, and purchase property on the south end of Lexington where most of the congregants lived. This was not financially a realistic plan and I knew it was not a wise move. The Conference Superintendent agreed with me so the church stayed where it was.

The attendance on my first Sunday was 27. The previous pastor did not use the platform or the pulpit to preach from and his services were more like a Sunday School class. My first Sunday as the new pastor, I preached from the pulpit. I began to pray for a revival to sweep the church as I shared a gospel message. After much prayer and a lot of hard work, within a few months the church had grown to 85. One Sunday our Conference Superintendent came to visit and told me he had never seen that many people in that Lexington church.

We saw people come to Jesus, become members and grow in their faith. At the same time the leaders of the church did everything possible to stop the growth of the church. They wanted my ministry to fail so they could sell the church and move out of the neighborhood.

One ministry that I started was a children's ministry. We had 25 children who would come to the church on Wednesday nights to sing, study and learn about Jesus. The children loved the ministry, were accepting Jesus as their Savior and were growing in their faith. That came to an abrupt end at one of our wonderful board meetings.

Monthly board meetings were a trial that taught me the importance of prayer. I never knew what was coming from the church board. They would take actions that would constantly hinder my ministry in any way possible. At one board meeting near the end of my first year, a motion was made to "get rid of the kids." I was shocked and asked how they could consider such a move. But the motion soon received a second and was approved unanimously. Their reasoning was that "the kids made too much noise and used up church supplies." I was told to "get rid of the kids" and if I did not, they would and they would not be as nice as I would be. This was only one of the many outrageous actions that the church board took to undermine my ministry.

One day I found myself sitting on the ground behind the church crying like a baby, asking God why these people were doing these awful things. I also told the Lord that I could not be a pastor and that I wanted out.

There have been a few times when Jesus has come and spoken to me so clearly that it was as if He were standing next to me. That day Jesus' message was very clear. He said, "Hal, if you don't keep your eyes on Me you will never make it." That was a day I will never forget. The words Jesus spoke to my heart that day have often come to mind when I am going through a difficult time.

As the end of my first year approached, I had decided to leave Lexington and return home to Michigan. I even spoke to a Conference Superintendent in Michigan about an appointment. When word got out to the church in Lexington, they called a meeting where I was treated like a king. After apologies and promises of a new attitude towards ministry and support of my ministry, I was persuaded to reconsider moving back to Michigan.

I was shocked by this move as I was so sure that they wanted me gone so they could follow through with their plans to sell and move. I thought maybe God had touched their hearts and I decided to give it another try. I decided to stay in Lexington for a second year.

Shortly after the conference year started, the church leaders returned to their old ways and I soon realized that I should have left after one year. In that denomination in 1973, pastors were appointed at the same time every year and it was very unusual to move from one church to another at any other time during the calendar year.

I felt trapped but I settled in realizing I had to wait another year before I could leave Lexington and head back to Michigan. I went into the fall determined to minister to the people in the surrounding neighborhood in any way possible. I began to make plans for the Thanksgiving and Christmas services. I so wanted to see God move in the little church in Lexington but continued to be met with opposition at every turn.

An example of this opposition was the church treasurer who lived on the south side of Lexington. He was very upset with the decision for the church to stay on the north side. I got paid $85 weekly and each Sunday I would ask the treasurer for my paycheck. Every Sunday he would tell me he had forgotten my check and I would find it in his mailbox on Monday morning. Every Monday I would drive across town to pick up my paycheck. It was his way of getting even.

I received a call one day from the conference treasurer who informed me that he did not have enough money to pay the Conference Superintendent. I was quite surprised and asked if he would like our church to take up a special offering. He informed me that our church had not paid our conference apportionments for several months. That money helped pay the Conference Superintendent's salary.

The church board had been told each month that all bills including the conference apportionments were paid in full. I immediately called a church board meeting and informed them of the call I had received. The board was upset and asked the treasurer why he had not paid the apportionments. He simply responded that the conference did not need our money and that he would not send them any money. The board overruled the treasurer and voted to pay all unpaid apportionments and send a letter of apology with a financial gift to the District Superintendent. The treasurer immediately resigned and left the church.

I mentioned earlier that I was very "cocky" during those early years of ministry. One Sunday I had a very humbling moment as we began our morning worship service. I strutted to the platform to sit in the big throne chair behind the pulpit. As I sat down, I felt a very sharp pain in my right thigh. I arose from the chair with a yell that would rival any Tarzan yell I ever let out in the junkyard in my childhood. I reached down and pulled an ½ inch upholstery tack from my thigh. The congregation was shocked by my yell and sat speechless. I looked around the sanctuary and spotted one of the teens laughing and I knew immediately that he had done it. His parents, both members of the church board, later made him apologize. I don't think I was as cocky after that experience and I always check out my chair before I am seated.

In spite of the attitudes of the church leadership, there were some meaningful experiences with the wonderful folks from the community around the church. One Sunday a young man named Albert James showed up at church. He was quiet and came to church alone.

Since my arrival as pastor, the church bell had not been rung. One Sunday Albert asked me why there was a rope hanging in the little lobby of the church. I told him it was there to ring the church bell. Albert asked if he could be the official bell ringer. I agreed and Albert rang the bell every Sunday for several months.

One Sunday as Albert was ringing the bell, something crashed in the little bell tower. I thought the bell was coming through the ceiling and was relieved when the ceiling held and no one was hurt. The bell never rang again while I served as pastor of the church. It seemed almost symbolic of the future of the church because of the negative attitudes of the church leaders.

Albert and I had several conversations concerning his relationship with Jesus. Albert was always very polite and seemed genuinely interested in knowing Jesus as his personal Savior. One Sunday I was in the middle of my sermon when Albert got up from his pew, walked forward and stood in front of the pulpit. I was not sure what to do. I glanced at the bulletin to see if I had missed something. I excused myself to the congregation in order to speak to Albert. I asked Albert if there was something I could do for him. He told me he wanted to accept Jesus as his Savior. I immediately asked for those who would like to pray with Albert to join me at the altar. That morning Albert James found forgiveness for his sins and received Jesus as his Savior and Lord.

I later asked Albert why he waited until I was in the middle of my sermon to come forward and ask for prayer. He told me that he had had a dream on Saturday night. In the dream Jesus came to him and told him to go forward in the middle of my sermon to receive Jesus as his Savior. Albert had been obedient and I was so glad. He did just what Jesus had instructed him to do.

Albert became a great blessing to the little church and God began to use him to touch his family. He began to pray for his mother and his brother, Danny to accept Jesus. We prayed for Albert's family every Sunday morning during our prayer time and God soon answered our prayers.

One Sunday following church, Albert told me he thought his brother and mother were ready to accept Jesus. I made an appointment to go to Albert's home that week and Albert began to prepare his mother and brother for my visit. After sharing the message of the Gospel with Albert's family, I ask Albert's brother, Danny if he would like to ask Jesus to be his Savior. He told me he would love to be a Christian. I was praising God in my heart and could hardly wait to pray.

When I asked Albert's Mom if she would like to receive Jesus as her Savior, she gave me an answer that I never expected. Mrs. James said, "I can't become a Christian because I am divorced." Mrs. James then began to tell me of years of abuse from her ex-husband including threats of death for her and her sons. Albert's Dad would put a gun to the heads of Albert and Danny and demand that Albert's Mom get on her knees and beg for their lives. This behavior happened repeatedly over a period of years until Mrs. James filed for divorce and got away from this abusive man. Mrs. James told me that she believed that if she had not escaped from her ex-husband, he would have killed them all.

Following the divorce, Mrs. James began to take her sons to counseling with a pastor in the neighborhood. During their first counseling session the pastor gave Mrs. James some bad news. He informed her that she had committed the unpardonable sin of divorce and that she could never be forgiven, know Jesus as her Savior or go to Heaven. WHAT?

After hearing this heartbreaking story, I took Mrs. James by the hands and told her that she could be a Christian and that Jesus wanted to be her Savior and was just waiting for her to invite Him into her life. I will never forget how Mrs. James began to cry as she expressed great joy at the Good News of God's unconditional love. Mrs. James, Danny, Albert and I bowed our heads in prayer and as we prayed, Albert's Mom and brother received Jesus as their Savior. It was a wonderful day of rejoicing and praise.

Mrs. James began to attend church every Sunday with her sons. The folks at the little church did not know what to think of her. One Sunday she stood to testify and a hush fell over the church. Mrs. James shared how she had been cleaning some drawers in her bedroom when she found a $100 bill. She said she did not need the money and believed God had given it to her to help someone with a special need. That week she ran into a neighbor walking down the sidewalk. The neighbor lady appeared to be so sad that Mrs. James asked what was wrong. Her neighbor shared that her husband was ill and she did not have the money to pay for the medication the doctor had prescribed. Mrs. James told the neighbor lady to come with her as she retrieved the $100 bill and put it into her neighbor's hand. She then told her neighbor that the money was from Jesus because He loved her so much. Then Mrs. James prayed with the lady and asked God for a special blessing for her husband's healing.

Albert and his family were a great blessing during my second year of ministry in Lexington. It was because of folks like the James family that I did not consider my ministry in Lexington a complete failure.

After that long, hard 2nd year, I decided to return to Michigan where I was appointed as the Associate Pastor of a Free Methodist Church in Pontiac, Michigan. My time in Lexington was very hard but it was a period of time when I learned a great deal about how to deal with adversity. I came out of Lexington stronger and wiser but I still had so much I needed to learn. My next classroom prepared by the Lord was in Pontiac, Michigan.

CHAPTER 13

A Time of Healing

In 1975, I was appointed to The First Free Methodist Church where I served with Rev. M.E. Andrews who had been a pastor almost 40 years. I was badly wounded by all that had happened to me in Lexington. Once again Jesus knew just what I needed to restore me and prepare me for many more years of ministry.

The folks of Pontiac First were kind and loving people and God did a great deal of healing in my life while I served there. I have always been grateful to the wonderful people of Pontiac First. They were a great encouragement to me during my brief ministry among them.

My ministry in Pontiac included preaching every Sunday, usually on Sunday nights. I also taught a teen Sunday School class, led youth meetings and directed the T.N.T. (Thursday Night Thing) program which involved a teen Bible study and recreation in the church gym.

I would go visiting door to door during the week, inviting families to send their children to Sunday School on the church bus. I rode the bus on Sunday and kept track of the attendance of each child.

Soon the bus was full of singing children and a few adults, who helped me with any problems that might arise among the over 50 children. If one of the children was absent, I would call or visit the family the next week. This special attention worked well to keep the children coming. Many of the children made commitments to Christ during my time as the "bus director."

A new ministry I started at Pontiac involved visiting nursing homes on Sunday afternoons. I would share the Sunday School lesson for that Sunday and give each attendee a copy of the Sunday School paper. Through this ministry, along with the bus ministry, we saw the Sunday School attendance double in just a few months.

One very funny memory I have from my time in Pontiac involved Rev. Andrews. He was preaching on a Sunday morning when he began to laugh loudly. We had a very elaborate pulpit that had a clock, a thermometer, and a barometer. Rev. Andrews happened to look down during his sermon and the barometer was pointing towards "dry and windy." When Rev. Andrews told everyone what was so funny, everyone joined in on the laughter.

While I was serving at Pontiac we had a "Bible Read-a-thon." The folks of the church signed up to come to the church and read the Bible aloud for 30 minutes. The reading continued until we had read the entire Bible, from Genesis to Revelation. The excitement grew as we neared the end of the Bible and many of the folks who had read returned to the church for the last minutes of reading. When the last chapter of Revelation was finished, a cheer arose from all who were present. We closed the time with prayer as we sensed a special visitation of the Holy Spirit.

I performed my first funeral while serving in Pontiac. Rev. Andrews had gone on vacation and a man, who was somehow connected with the church, passed away. I arrived at the funeral home an hour before the service as a very nervous "funeral rookie." I kept asking God what to say about a man I had never met and expected that this would be a very short service. As I sat praying, the funeral director came in to let me know I had 5 minutes before the service time. He then said, "He sure was a wonderful man." When I realized that he knew the deceased gentleman, I asked what he knew about the man. As the funeral director shared I took notes and in 5 minutes I gathered a lot of information for the service.

When the funeral service was over, the family complimented me on performing a good service. They were especially impressed with how well I knew the deceased man. It meant so much to the family that I had made the service so personal and that I had honored the man's life.

Since that time, I have attempted to always meet with the families of deceased persons to gather information about their lives. This simple gesture has been met with gratitude so many times by family members and friends of the persons who have passed away.

Another lesson I learned while in Pontiac was to be myself when preaching a sermon. We had a gentleman in the congregation who was the vice-president of a local university. One week, in order to impress him, I decided to try to preach an "intellectual sermon." I do not consider myself any kind of an intellectual and the sermon was a total failure. As I was preaching the special "intellectual sermon" I looked around the sanctuary and noticed many heads down, including the university vice-president, as a spirit of deep sleep swept across the congregation. I was so embarrassed that I decided that I would never try to do that again.

One of the life changing miracles I witnessed while serving in Pontiac took place in the life of Mr. Bob Highfield. Bob was in Crittenden Hospital in Rochester, Michigan, in the final stages of cancer. He had been told he did not have long to live.

Rev. Andrews went out of state and one of my duties while he was gone was to go to Crittenden Hospital every day to visit and pray with Bob. I set my schedule around visiting Bob and it turned out to be well worth the effort.

After the first week of visits with him, Bob told me he needed to "get something off his chest" and asked if he could confess something to me. I told Bob that I had no power to forgive sin but I would be glad to listen.

Bob began to share something that had happened over 50 years before. The guilt he had carried all those years began to pour out. When he finished his confession, he told me that he felt better. I suggested to Bob that if he felt better having told me, when I could not forgive him, he would feel so much better if he told Jesus, who could forgive him. Bob said, "That's a good idea." Then he started to talk to Jesus, telling Him just what he had told me. When Bob finished his confession to Jesus, I led him in a prayer asking Jesus to forgive all of his sins and to come into his heart as his Savior. Following the prayer time, Bob began to cry. We hugged each other and I left the hospital praising God for the miracle I had just witnessed.

Bob's wife called me that evening following her visit with her husband. She said to me, "I don't know what you did to my husband today but I would appreciate it if you would go back and do it again tomorrow." She then told me that that day was the first time she had seen her husband smile in months. Bob was a forgiven man. He Knew Christ's forgiveness and was now ready to face death with the promise of eternal life filling his heart.

I continued to visit Bob even after Rev. Andrews came home. A week or so after Rev. Andrews got home, Bob Highfield went to Heaven. At Bob's funeral there was much talk about Heaven because we knew that Bob was there enjoying eternal life. To this day I look forward to seeing Bob again when I get to Heaven.

Another miracle that took place while serving in Pontiac was the news that I was going to be a father. I was so excited that in February of 1976, my wife was due to give birth to our first child. Little did I know that before the birth of my first child, I would face death in one of the great crises in my life- "Typhoid Fever."

Daddy in his Army uniform

Daddy with his guitar, 1950

Grandma Langston 1960

Uncle Don (Pop), Daddy, Shoe (Grandpa Phillips), Julie, Grandma Phillips, Uncle Aubry and Uncle Sam

Me at about 6 mos old

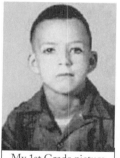
My 1st Grade picture

Me, Julie and Eddie 1956

Eddie, Julie, Mama and me, 1987

Me, Mom, Donnie and
Eddie ready for church
1964

Mom and Pop

The "God Squad" from
Asbury College, 1970

My wedding to Kathy (Princing) Woods
Kathy's Dad, Kathy's mom, Kathy, me,
Sarah, Stephanie, Stephen and Jason

My family, Children and grandchildren, 2012

Stephen in his
truck 2013

Me and Kathy

Kathy and me (back row on the right)
with our grandchildren at the lake
4th of July 2014

CHAPTER 14

Typhoid Fever

The summer of 1975 proved to be one of the most difficult of my life. I had preached at a family church camp near Kingston, Ontario the summer of 1974. As a result of having a good camp experience, I was invited to come back in 1975.

The 1975 camp was going very well, although it was unusually hot that summer. I remember drinking a lot of water from a drinking fountain near the dining hall.

When the camp was concluded, I said my good-byes to many new friends that I had made during the ten day camp and I headed home to Michigan. Little did I know that the camp would change my life in ways that I never dreamed of.

I arrived at home in Pontiac, Michigan, where I was serving as Associate pastor of the First Free Methodist Church. I was home for one week before I packed my bags to head out to another camp in Michigan.

It was late July and the East Michigan Conference of the Free Methodist Church had the large Bethel Park camp meeting just west of Flint, Michigan. I was asked to serve as youth director for the camp meeting. I was excited for the opportunity to serve my conference in this way.

A few days after the camp meeting started, I began to feel sick. I would wake up in the night with night sweats, stomach cramps, and severe chills. After three days of this sickness, I knew I had to get help.

I drove to McLaren Hospital in Flint in the middle of the night and asked for help in the emergency room. After examining me from head to foot including a chest x-ray, the doctor thought I had pneumonia. I was admitted to the hospital and more lab tests were performed to confirm a diagnosis for my illness.

I was so sick that all I wanted to do was sleep. My roommate wanted to talk, but I was not able to stay awake long enough to hold a very long conversation. My illness continued to baffle the doctors for two more days and I continued to get worse. None of the test results were conclusive for a diagnosis.

On my third day in the hospital, everything changed. Two nurses dressed in gowns, masks and gloves came into my room and began to move my belongings to another room. Soon, two other nurses came in dressed the same way and moved my roommate's bed into the hallway. They returned and took me from the room and began pushing me down the hallway. I asked one of the nurses where we were going. She told me I was going into a single room. When I asked why, she told me I had to be put in isolation. The word "isolation" scared me and I demanded an explanation as to why such a radical action was being taken. At that point, one of the nurses told me that I had been diagnosed with Typhoid Fever.

I had heard of Typhoid Fever, mostly from old movies on television and stories from senior citizens. In almost every case the people who had Typhoid Fever died because there was no cure. And it was apparent to me that several of the hospital staff had seen some of the same movies and heard similar stories because there were nurses that refused to enter my room for fear that they might catch the deadly disease.

During the next month in the hospital very few people came to see me. Most of my family members stayed away. The pastor I served under and my conference superintendent even stayed away. Their concern about contracting the disease left me feeling alone and deserted. Even my wife stayed away because she was pregnant and the doctors advised her not to visit me. I don't know what I would have done if not for the kindness of one man.

That man was Rev. Henry Schmidt. He was the minister of visitation at the Davison Free Methodist Church about 25 miles from the hospital. Rev. Schmidt came to see me almost every day during my month in McLaren Hospital. He prayed with me, encouraged me, and read to me from the Bible. When this dear man walked through the door of my room dressed in gown, mask and gloves, it was as if God had sent an angel to minister to me. I will always be grateful for the kindness shown to me by Rev. Schmidt.

While I was in the hospital I learned that I was not the only person who had contracted Typhoid Fever. There were 36 other people who had attended the family church camp in Canada that were also very ill.

In Kingston, Ontario, an entire floor of a hospital had been set-aside for Typhoid patients. Needless to say, the health department in Ontario started a full investigation. The result was that the family church camp was closed down. I had preached the last service that was ever held at the 100-year-old camp

At the Bethel Park Camp in Michigan, the health department did an investigation and the result of their investigation showed that there were many areas in this camp that were in violation of health codes. The camp was given a limited license for the next year and then the camp was closed. I do believe I may be the only preacher to close two camps in one summer.

After a month in McLaren Hospital in Flint, I was released to go home to Pontiac. It was so good to be home. I was 20 pounds lighter and much weaker physically, but I was home and I could not have been happier. Little did I know that my stay at home would be very short.

Less than two weeks after I came home from the hospital, I began to feel sick again. I did everything to convince myself that I was coming down with the flu or that I was suffering from food poisoning or anything else I could think of except Typhoid Fever. Finally, just as before, I went to the emergency room in the middle of the night. I had not even been home two weeks and it was starting all over again. The only difference was that this time would be much worse than the first.

Upon arriving at St. Joseph Mercy Hospital in Pontiac, they began to examine me by taking my temperature. The nurse was shocked to see that my temperature was 105.6 and immediately found a doctor to continue the examination. With the knowledge that an adult can have brain damage with a temperature of 105, the doctor acted immediately and gave instructions to get my temperature down. I was taken to a room, put in isolation and packed in ice.

Bags of ice were brought and put around me in the bed. I was so cold that my body shook uncontrollably from chills related to the fever. After a while I fell asleep but as I awoke, the cold was so sharp it felt like knives poking my skin.

My doctor came to my room shortly after I awoke to check on my condition. He found that one of the bags of ice had leaked onto my bed and I was lying in a water soaked bed. He was not happy.

The treatment for Typhoid started right away. The diagnosis was that I had a relapse and the disease was back with more punch than the first time around. I was put in isolation and anyone who came near me had to wear a mask, a gown and gloves. My nightmare was back and a sense of hopelessness overwhelmed me.

For the next three weeks my doctor did everything he could to stop the Typhoid from ravaging my body, but nothing seemed to help. I only grew worse hour by hour.

Different things began to happen to me this time that had not happened in my first go-around with Typhoid. A friend from my church came to see me. As my friend Tom stood at the foot of my bed, I was surprised that Tom had a twin brother with him! I asked Tom to introduce me to his brother. He abruptly left the room and brought a nurse back with him. His concern was that no one else had been in the room with him and he definitely did not have a twin brother. I was having double vision.

Another time, my doctor came to check on me. Dr. Hallet had long sideburns and dark wavy hair. I was convinced that he was Elvis Presley. Now I was hallucinating. I thanked Elvis for coming to see me in the hospital. Then I asked Elvis to sing me a song. Dr. Hallet touched my face and asked if I knew my name, I answered "My name is Hal Phillips and I'm so glad you came to see me, Elvis!"

The next day Dr. Hallet told my family that he did not know what else to do to get my temperature under control. He said that if something did not happen, I might die. Mom got the prayer chain going.

In an effort to keep my temperature down, my clothes were all taken away and I was put between plastic thermo blankets through which cold alcohol was pumped. My body would shake from the chill until I'd fall asleep. When I would awake, I would begin to shake again. It was the most miserable experience that I'd ever known, and I began to realize that I was losing hope of coming out of this experience alive.

I began to pray that God would let me die quickly if I was not going to recover. I decided it would be easier for all concerned, my family, my church and me if I just died quickly. But thank God, in spite of my prayers to die, He had another plan. It was a plan greater than I could dream of, especially in the hopeless condition I was in.

The day finally came when I reached my limit. I had been in the thermo blankets for several days. The shaking from the chill had brought great pain in my abdomen and back and I could no longer feel my legs. When a nurse came in to check my temperature I begged her to let me out of the blankets for just five minutes. She was very reluctant but after much pleading she agreed. Another nurse joined her and as one took my temperature the other nurse removed the upper thermo blanket. The nurses helped me up so I could sit on the edge of my bed. Before they left the room they told me my temperature was almost 103. The nurses told me that I could only sit up for five minutes and then they would put me back under the thermo blankets.

As the nurses left the room, I began to call out to God as I had never called out to Him before. I told Him I could not take anymore. I was losing my mind and without His help, I was going to die.

Then I claimed I Corinthians 10:13, "There is no temptation (or trial) that has overtaken you, but that which is common to all mankind, but God is faithful and will not allow you to be tempted (or tested) beyond what we could bear but will with the temptation (or trial) provide a way of escape that we may be able to bear it." I wept as I prayed as I felt this was my last hope. I laid back down and fell asleep.

As I slept, one of the nurses returned and began to put me back into the thermo blankets. I asked her to take my temperature, for I believed God had touched me. After much pleading, she reluctantly put the thermometer in my mouth.

When the nurse took the thermometer from my mouth, she looked at it, shook it, and put it back in my mouth. The second time she took the thermometer from my mouth she looked at it and walked out of the room. She returned with another nurse who took my temperature for a third time – and then a fourth. My temperature was 98.6! Praise God!!

The nurses shook their heads in disbelief at what was happening. They told me that they did not understand why or how this happened, but my temperature was now normal. The thermo blankets were removed from my bed. I was allowed to put on some clothes and was given a warm blanket. My temperature did not go up again. God had healed me. I was well! I fell asleep, and slept like a baby.

The next day when my doctor came in, he told me that he did not understand what had happened but was so glad that it had. He told me how concerned he was because he had done all he could. I shared with Dr. Hallet how I had prayed and claimed I Corinthians 10: 13, and believed God had healed me. He just smiled and shook his head. I don't believe he understood, but I knew he was glad I was well.

Dr. Hallet wanted to make sure the Typhoid Fever had not done damage to my organs, especially my gall bladder. He sent me for x-rays to examine my gall bladder and told me that my gall bladder might have to be removed.

I prayed that God would heal my gall bladder if there were problems so I would not have to have surgery. I went for my x-rays and when the results came back everything was normal.

A few days later I packed my bags and headed home for good. I was now 40 pounds lighter than I was before I got Typhoid Fever. It was so good to be home, but I still had some problems to overcome.

I had been in isolation for two months and I had a terrible time moving back into a normal schedule. I did not want to leave the house and would even draw the drapes and sit in the dark.

Dr. Hallet set an appointment to see me a week after I was discharged from the hospital. I told him how I was feeling and he asked if there was anything coming up that I could get out of the house for short periods of time. I told him that my brother was preaching revival services at a church in Flint about 50 miles away. He told me that he was prescribing for me to go to the revival. That night I drove to Flint to hear my brother preach and that fear of being around people went away and never returned.

Another problem I had was drugs. The doctor gave me a prescription for pain pills and sleeping pills with several refills on each prescription. I took the pills for three days just before I went to bed. The first night I felt I was floating on a cloud of ecstasy and I liked that feeling. The second night I got the same high I had the first night and I still enjoyed it, but I also became concerned. I knew what was happening was dangerous. I remembered the drug addiction of my mother and I knew that I was vulnerable also.

The next day I spend some time praying that God would protect me from addiction to the drugs. God answered that prayer right away. That night when I took pills I did not float and I did not feel high. Instead, I had what I can only describe as a "bad trip". I felt as if my head was going to explode. I passed back and forth through the parsonage like a caged animal for almost two hours before this awful experience finally came to an end. I fell on my knees in the dark and thanked God I was still alive and I promised Him I would not take another one of those pills. Minutes later I flushed all the pills and tore up the prescriptions. That was the end of my drug trips. God took over and helped me deal with the pain and helped me sleep. I did not need the drugs at all. God had performed another miracle for me.

The last problem I had was the hospital bills that were not paid by my insurance. The folks who lived in Canada had all their medical expenses covered by their national health plan. I was the only American to get sick and my insurance did not pay all the bills. When my Christian friends in Canada learned of my financial distress, they took up offerings in their churches and sent me the money they had collected. All my bills were paid in full due to the loving generosity of my Canadian brothers and sisters in Christ.

As I write this chapter, it has been over twenty-five years since I had Typhoid Fever. I still look back at that experience as one of the great spiritual growth events of my life. One friend asked me if I felt I was the same Christian now that I was before I got sick. I told him I am now 10 times the Christian I was before Typhoid Fever became a part of my life story.

As I close this chapter I think of Rev. Harry Schmidt who was so faithful to visit me during my first hospital stay. Before Typhoid Fever I had very little sympathy for people who were sick and I hated to visit hospitals, maybe because of the way my mother was when I was growing up. Following my Typhoid episode, I have a new found compassion for those who are suffering from illness. Visiting people in the hospital became a top priority for me and has been for twenty-five years. I attribute this change to the memory of how awful it was to be so sick and to the wonderful ministry of Rev. Henry Schmidt.

Truly, Romans 8:28 is true when it says "All things work together for good to those who love God and are called according to his purpose."

CHAPTER 15

Pleasant View

The weeks following my two months in the hospital with typhoid fever were difficult. I had a very hard time getting back in the swing of things, as I had very little contact with people and had been alone the vast majority of the time during the months of sickness.

During my hospital stay I had turned 25 years old but there was no celebration as I was so close to death. The folks from the Pontiac Church had a party for me and that helped to revive my spirits. Because of the wonderful love of my church family, I slowly but surely I got back into a regular schedule of preaching, visiting and eating. As a result, I began to regain some of the 40 pounds that I lost to the typhoid fever. That was not hard as I love to eat.

Some people were hesitant, even months later, to get close to me for fear that I might still be contagious. I was so grateful to be alive and in ministry that I was very patient with the folks who had stood by me so faithfully.

As we came to the end of 1975, I was excited for our first child to be born around the first of February 1976. I so looked forward to being a dad. This was a great blessing and helped to lift my spirits more than anything else could have.

I was surprised in December when I received a call from our Conference Superintendent, who asked if he could come to see me. As we sat in my office he told me of a church in the thumb of Michigan about 50 miles north of Pontiac that had lost their pastor. My superintendent asked if I would be willing to become their pastor. I shared that it would be difficult as my wife was due February 1st. He agreed and said that if I was willing to move, I would be appointed to be the new pastor March 1st, 1976. I asked if I could visit the church and town before I gave him a final decision. The following week, we met at the church and as we walked through the beautiful building, I felt God speak to me to come and be the pastor of the Pleasant View Free Methodist Church in Mayville, Michigan. "Pleasant View" came from the beautiful view of open farmland and sunsets to the west of the church property.

The Pontiac Church was informed by the Conference Superintendent in January of 1976, and we began to make plans to move to Mayville. Those plans had to take a backseat until the birth of our beautiful daughter.

Sarah Elizabeth Phillips was born on February 10, 1976 and I was so blessed to be a father. As soon as Sarah was born, she was laid in a metal tray. I walked over to her and said, "Hi Sarah Elizabeth. I'm your Dad." Her response was to let out a cry that sounded more like a scream but I knew that deep in her heart she was glad to be my daughter.

Because Sarah weighed 10 lbs. 1 oz. she was placed in the neonatal Intensive Care until some test were run to make sure she was not diabetic. All of the tests came back good and it was decided that she was a just big, healthy baby girl. We were all home in a few days preparing to move to our new appointment in Mayville.

Our move was scheduled on March 4, 1976. On March 3, 1976, Michigan experienced the worst ice storm in its history. The moving van came on the 3rd to begin loading our things. Soon it began to rain and the rain began to freeze. We finished loading the truck in the late afternoon and planned to leave early the next morning for the 50 mile trip north to Mayville.

As we began to travel north, the ice damage grew much worse and before we reached Mayville, power lines were all down along the highway. Trees were uprooted everywhere. The only time since then I have ever witnessed anything like it, was when I visited Florida after Hurricane Charlie.

When we arrived at the parsonage, there was no electricity, no running water and no heat in the house. The movers began to unload the truck and I began to pray about what we were going to do as there was no way we could stay in that church parsonage. My prayers were answered when Roland and Reba O'Brien parked in front of the parsonage and came knocking on the door. When I answered the door, this couple in their sixties met me with huge smiles and welcomed me as their new pastor. After helping us put a few things away, they informed us that we were going with them to their house to stay until the power and water were back on. God answered my prayer in His perfect way.

The O'Brien's lived in a home on Pero Lake near Lapeer, Michigan. Their home was about 20 miles from the church. They had power, water and heat at their house and made us feel very much at home in our time of need. As time went along, and as Sarah grew older, Roland and Reba became Grandpa Rolly and Grandma Reba. This wonderful couple became a great blessing to our lives and we loved them as if they were part of our family.

On March 7, 1976, I led my first worship service at the Pleasant View Church. There was still no electricity so someone brought a generator and hooked it up to the furnace so we could have heat in the sanctuary. At worship time it was about 60 degrees in the sanctuary. I often joked with the folks that they had given my family a cool reception as their new pastor.

Within two weeks the power and water were restored to Mayville. My family moved back to the church parsonage and we began to establish a regular daily schedule for our lives.

The Pleasant View Church was hurting badly as a result of the loss of their pastor. The former pastor had not died but had become very angry with the church. He had said many hurtful things to the people of the congregation. He would say things before the services, in his sermons and even as people were leaving to go home following the services. As a result, over one half of the regular attendees had left the church and many never came back. I had a lot of praying and work to do.

One of the reasons that the former pastor was upset with the church was the condition of the parsonage. He and his wife refused to unpack many of their belongings and finally decided to move back to their home in the suburbs of Detroit.

When I arrived, a building committee had already been formed and plans were in place to build a new parsonage as soon as the weather broke. When the time came, we broke ground next to the church building and the first building program of my ministry was underway.

Our plan was to put the old parsonage up for sale and use the money from the sale to help finish the new parsonage. The only problem was the sale of the old parsonage happened much faster than anyone envisioned. The folks who wanted to purchase the house also wanted immediate occupancy which meant my family had to find a place to live until the new parsonage was completed.

The church's solution to the dilemma was to move our furniture into the finished garage of the new parsonage and to move my family into a travel trailer in the yard of one of the members. My wife, baby girl and I lived in the travel trailer for six weeks. This was very hard but well worth the wait, when finally in July of 1976, we moved into the beautiful new parsonage.

The Pleasant View Church was a part of the East Michigan Conference of the Free Methodist Church. The conference had a monthly paper called the "Voice. On the back page of the paper the churches of the conference were listed from top to bottom according to largest increase in attendance to greatest loss compared to the year before. Because of the turmoil that preceded my arriving at Pleasant View, our church was dead last in attendance gains (losses) for 27 straight months.

I began to pray for revival. I visited many people each week and I preached my heart out as I stayed true to the teachings of Scripture. In spite of all my prayers and efforts, the Pleasant View Church was still last in attendance gains for over two years. It was one of the most difficult times in my ministry as the thoughts of failure plagued my mind.

In the midst of my battle with feelings of failure, God in His goodness sent me a surprise that I did not expect. In early March of 1977, my wife became very sick with nausea and after a week or so decided to go to the doctor. She came home from the doctor's office with surprising news. She was pregnant and I was going to be a father for the second time.

On November 16, 1977, Stephen Paul Phillips was born at the Lapeer General Hospital in Lapeer, Michigan. Stephen was a big boy like his sister, weighing in at 9 lbs. 14 oz. After some concern, he was determined to be a very healthy baby boy. Stephen was a surprise baby but he came at a time when I needed something to get my mind off my seeming failure as a pastor.

It was also during those early years at Pleasant View Church that my Grandmother Phillips, Nanny, as we fondly called her, passed away in late 1978. Nanny had raised my sister, Julie and took Eddie and me into her very small home before we moved to Michigan.

I returned to Arkansas for Nanny's funeral and while there I visited my mother, my step-father and the cemeteries where many of my loved ones were buried. At my grandmother's funeral service, my brothers Eddie and Donny and I sang my grandmother's favorite song, "This World Is Not My Home." We all cried as Nanny was laid to rest but were so happy to know she was in Heaven. Nanny had accepted Jesus as her Savior and was baptized just one month before she died. This was a great answer to prayer for all of us as we had prayed for my grandmother's salvation for many years. I believe the trip back to Arkansas was a good reminder of where the Lord had brought me from and gave me a renewed spirit as I returned to my ministry at the Pleasant View Church.

After over two years of praying, preaching, visiting and teaching God's truth, something began to happen in the Pleasant View Church. Slowly the oppressive spirit that had permeated the church began to lift. I believed the Holy Spirit was truly reviving the church and I was so excited. New folks began to come to church and some who had left over two years before began to return.

One of the folks who began coming to Pleasant View Church was a man named Don. I first met him when he came to the back door of our parsonage. I asked why he came to the back door and he informed me that he could not read or write and was not worthy to come to the front door. I assured Don he was as worthy as anyone else. I told him he could come to our front door and visit our home anytime. I also invited him to come and visit our church. Don was an excellent mechanic and did much work on my cars through the years. Don and his wife began to attend the church, made commitments to Christ and became new members. Don served on the board of trustees for several years. Don and his wife were great blessings to the church.

God's blessing was so great that the Pleasant View Church went from last to first in attendance growth. In 1979, the Pleasant View Church was the "Church Of The Year" in the East Michigan Conference. The "Church Of The Year" was given to the church in our conference with the greatest growth in attendance and membership. The Pleasant View Church had doubled in size by the time I was appointed to my next church. God had answered prayer and brought revival as *2 Chronicles 7:14* promises. God is faithful. Praise God's holy Name.

My years at Pleasant View were not easy but were blessed, as I was able to see God's power at work in renewing and reviving the church. The folks at Pleasant View were kind and loving and helped me to see that God could work in the most difficult circumstances to bring glory to His holy name.

After 5 years at Pleasant View, I was appointed to the Countryside Free Methodist Church in Sandusky, Michigan. God had more lessons for me to learn and a new classroom. In 1980, I headed to Sandusky with my little family to find out what God had in store for me there.

CHAPTER 16

Countryside

The Countryside Free Methodist Church had an interesting history that made it very unique. The church was a merger of four small Free Methodist Churches. The churches were the Elmer, Sandusky, Carsonville and Ball Free Methodist Churches. Each of the churches was over 100 years old and it was not easy for folks to see their church close for the merger.

On a given Sunday in 1975, the four churches were to take a vote on whether they supported the merger into what would be the Countryside Free Methodist Church. If all four of the churches voted to merge, the individual churches would be sold and a new church would be built on a new five acre parcel of land purchased by the conference. Three of the churches were highly in favor of the merger and there was no doubt about how they would vote. The Ball Free Methodist Church was opposed to the merger and had let it be known that they would not support the merger and the building of the new church.

Mr. Howard Orchard, a leading member of the Ball Church, told me of the events of that crucial Sunday morning. Howard went to the old church building on Sunday morning to start a fire in the woodstove to warm up the building for the morning worship service. Howard then returned home and had breakfast with his wife. As he was washing the breakfast dishes, he looked out of the kitchen window to see the Ball Church in flames. The church burned to the ground that morning.

Later that day the members of the Ball Church voted unanimously to support the merger and the Countryside Free Methodist Church was born.

Every time I tell this story, I always think of the old saying, "God works in mysterious ways His wonders to perform."

The very first service held at the Countryside church had double the attendance of the four small churches combined. The new church continued to grow to the point that even before the dedication of the new church, new footings had been poured for the expansion of the sanctuary. Another church expansion and a beautiful parsonage were built just a few years before my family arrived in Sandusky.

My appointment to be the pastor of the Countryside Church was different than my other appointments. There was secrecy about the move from Pleasant View to Countryside. I had not experienced that before and to this day I still do not understand why. The possibility of being moved to Countryside was mentioned to me by the conference superintendent but never confirmed. Because of that, my assumption was that I was returning to Pleasant View for another year.

On conference Sunday 1980, when my name was read as the new pastor of the Countryside Church, there was a gasp across the conference floor. The Pleasant View folks were shocked that I was leaving them. The Countryside folks were surprised that I was coming as their new pastor. And I was stunned by both events.

The only idea that I have come up with for the secrecy was that the conference superintendent had someone else in mind to go to Countryside and that plan fell through at the last minute and I was "plan B." Whatever happened, God placed me at Countryside and I was blessed to be their pastor for the next seven years.

I was amazed that I had come so far from those difficult days in Lexington to be appointed the pastor of the largest church in Sandusky, Michigan, at the age of 29. God had richly blessed my ministry and a big part of that was the lesson I learned early on to keep my eyes on Jesus and not focus on people. God is good all the time!

During my first year at Countryside, the church board came to realize that we did not have enough staff to care for the needs of the church. On Wednesday evenings that first year, I would meet with 25 to 30 teens in the parsonage basement for 30 minutes of Bible study. The teens would then go to the church gym for recreation for the second part of the hour. I would go to the sanctuary to lead the adult Bible study after one of the folks led the singing and prayer time. It almost seems comical now, but at that time it is what needed to be done.

The church voted to hire an associate pastor and asked if I knew anyone whom I would like to work with. My mind went directly to Del Covington, who was a member of the Pontiac Church. Del had received the call to ministry and was seeking God's will about his future. I began to pray about asking Del to come and work with me and God seemed to confirm to me that Del was the man for the job.

I contacted the conference superintendent and asked permission to ask Del Covington to join our church staff. Upon receiving approval from the conference, I contacted Del and he enthusiastically agreed to join our team at Countryside.

The church had purchased a house that adjoined the church property. Within a few months Del, his wife Sherry and their son Stephen moved in and began to work with us in ministry. Since Del's son was named Stephen and so was mine, it created a small problem. We solved it by calling Del's son Stephen Ray and my son Stephen Paul. The boys became best friends and Stephen Paul spoke fondly of Stephen Ray through the years to come.

We had a wonderful secretary at Countryside by the name of Ruthann Walker who continued to serve when I began my ministry there. Ruthann and her husband Harry became very close friends and at one time even offered to adopt me as their own son.

Ruthann would come in every morning and brew a pot of coffee in her original Mr. Coffee. I had never been a coffee drinker but the smell of the coffee was so nice. One day I asked Ruthann if I could have a cup and she graciously agreed. Since that day I have rarely gone a morning without a cup of coffee to help start my day.

Ruthann typed the first draft of this book for me in 1987 on an I.B.M. typewriter. That first edition of the book had a green cover with a red door on it. I distributed over 1,000 copies of the old green book and I still have a few original copies lying around. Thank you, Ruthann.

I remember one day as I entered the church, Ruthann was parked in the "no parking-loading zone" in front of the church. I took out a piece of paper and wrote her a $100 parking ticket. The next day I found an envelope on my desk with $100 in play money to pay for Ruthann's ticket. I felt the money was not mine so I wrote her name on the envelope and placed it in the offering plate the next Sunday. Ruthann told me she saw the envelope in the offering plate as it passed her in the pew and wondered why an envelope with her name was in the offering. On Sunday afternoon the treasurer called her to ask why she would put play money in the offering. The treasurer did not think it was funny but I sure got a kick out of hearing the story on Monday during our weekly staff meeting.

Ruthann and I almost always got along but there was one time when Ruthann really got mad at me. Countryside had a preschool and daycare center that employed about a dozen people. As pastor, I was the executive director and had the power to hire and fire employees. I did not like that part of the job but it was part of the job description as pastor of the church. The reason Ruthann was so upset was because I was considering hiring a person to work at the preschool that she highly objected to. She gave her opinion why I was wrong and I shared mine why I felt it was right. I then hired the person in spite of Ruthann's objection.

Shortly afterwards, Pastor Del went to Ruthann's office and found dozens of pencils all over her floor. Del told her that she had dropped some of her pencils. She informed him that she did not drop them but threw them in frustration with me. Del picked up the pencils and immediately came to me urging a peace treaty between Ruthann and myself. Within a few days the crisis was over and we were able to laugh at the incident. We are still laughing at it to this day.

Every fall we had a Sunday School contest to help grow our Sunday School attendance. One year we decided to have two teams "the Hatfields" and "the McCoys," famous for the great feud in the 1800's. One of the men in the church somehow found a bearskin coat and wore it to church for the Sunday School contest. Later that night I had to go over to the church to get something out of Ruthann's office. When I unlocked her office door this terrible smell hit me. As I turned on the light in the dark office, I saw the bearskin coat thrown over a chair next to the door. I don't think I screamed but I do know that my feet left the floor and it was a miracle that I did not have a heart attack right there. To this day I wonder if Ruthann left that coat there for me to find in the middle of the night.

God blessed our ministry at Countryside and with much work and lots of prayer, the church grew. In November 1982, we averaged 285 in morning worship. That was a highpoint because that month we had the highest attendance of any church in the East Michigan Conference of the Free Methodist Church. God is indeed good, all the time.

God was blessing our church and my ministry but at the same time I was entering a personal crisis which would prove to be one of the most difficult times of my ministry. I entered into a period of depression that was like a deep valley of darkness. I had gone through short periods of depression, especially around Thanksgiving and Christmas. Several of my family members had passed away during November and December, and I believe this was a trigger for the feelings of depression. The most obvious of these deaths was my death of my father on December 2, 1952.

Usually I would go into this difficult time in the late fall and pull out of it after the beginning of the year. The fall of 1983 was different. As the leaves began to fall and the cool temperature began to overtake the warmth of summer, I could feel my spirit beginning to fall. I prayed, studied my

Bible, attended Bible studies and never missed a church service but the depression just got worse. It became almost unbearable!

I had an appointment with my family doctor for a sore throat and sinus infection that seemed to be an annual event. After his examination, he asked if there was anything else he could help me with. I told him about how I was feeling. The Dr. asked a few questions and wrote a prescription for an antidepressant and recommended that I call a friend of his who was a counselor.

The next day I called the counselor and made an appointment. A week later I was in the counselor's office hoping to find some relief from the sadness I was experiencing. The counselor asked me to tell him about my life and I told him everything from my childhood to the present. I think it took a month of 45 minute sessions to get through everything. During the sessions, the counselor said very little.

After several weeks of pouring out my soul, I asked the counselor if he could help me. He then told me that he had served as the intake director of a psychiatric hospital for several years, but had never heard of a childhood as bad as mine. He then told me that I had a hole in my soul that was "infinite" and that he did not know if he could help me, but wanted me to continue to meet with him and he would try. My childhood had caught up with me and I did not know what to do.

Several weeks later I was no better and the medicine the doctor gave me just made me groggy. I became unable to sleep and felt that I was on a downward spiral. I became concerned that if I could not get a hold of this, it might be the end of my ministry. Then one night God gave me a very special miracle.

It was late at night and I had gone to the church sanctuary to pray. I left all the lights off except the light behind the cross on the front wall behind the pulpit. As I lay on the floor of the sanctuary, I cried out to the Lord for help and hope for the future. I was desperate for God to help me and the tears flowed as I pleaded for mercy in my time of trial. Then something happened that I cannot explain except to say, it was a miracle.

As I lay on my face before the cross crying, I heard someone singing. It was a deep voice, like a baritone or a bass singer in a quartet and it was beautiful. The words I heard were, "Fear thou not for I'll be with thee, I will still thy Pilot be. Never mind the tossing billows, take my hand and trust in me."

I arose to my feet thinking someone had entered the church and had heard me crying and decided to sing a song to encourage me.... but there was no one there. I began a search of the building. I checked every room including the closets and discovered that I was alone in the church building, or was I? I came to the conclusion after the extensive search, it was a singing angel, sent by God, to encourage me in my time of need. After these many years I am still convinced that God sent an angel to sing me a song.

I did not tell anyone about this experience for years for fear I would be thought to have had a hallucination like I did when I was sick with typhoid fever. It was a secret between God and me until years later, when the Lord gave me confirmation through a wonderful pastor's wife in the state of Pennsylvania.

Within a week of my encounter with the angel, I was sitting in my office looking toward my bookshelf and noticed a book that I had purchased some time before but had never read. It was a book by Dr. David Seamands, who was my pastor during my years at Asbury College. The book was entitled, "Putting Away Childish Things." I picked the book up and began to thumb through the chapters. That is when I saw a chapter entitled "Healing of Memories" and I knew this was an answer to my prayers.

In this chapter, Dr. Seamands shared a prayer therapy that would help to bring healing for terrible things that have happened in our past. I began to read the chapter and believed this was what I needed to bring healing to my life. God witnessed to me that day "the infinite hole in my soul" could be filled by God's infinite love. What a great load was lifted from my mind as God spoke to me. I felt hope for the first time in months.

I was so excited that I took the book to my next counseling session and read it to the counselor for the entire 45 minute session. When the time was over, he told me that this might work and to begin the prayer therapy right away. He then charged me $75 for the session.

I did begin the prayer therapy the next day and continued it every day for several weeks. Slowly but surely God began to bring healing to my memories of childhood trauma. After a few months, I found that there was no depression related to the memories that had plagued me. God had healed me and the memories I once could not speak of without much pain, I could now speak of with freedom and peace. Hallelujah!

My ministry at Countryside lasted for seven years from 1980-1987. During those seven years, the United States went through a severe recession. Many of the families in the farming community lost their farms and moved from the area. One day I sat down and listed all the people connected with the Countryside Church who had left the area. I listed over 100 names. In spite of the loss of so many folks, the church continued an effective ministry.

In 1983, Pastor Del and I were invited to a luncheon at the Presbyterian Church to hear a special speaker who had begun several organizations called "Project Blessing" in the thumb of Michigan, to provide food and clothing to those in need. At the close of the speaker's presentation, he walked straight to me and asked, "Will you help start a Project Blessing in Sandusky?" I felt every eye in the room staring at me as I stammered, "I will try."

At our next Ministerial Association meeting, Pastor Del and I took a proposal to begin a Project Blessing in Sandusky. In our proposal we suggested that we call our organization by a different name than the communities around us. We recommended the name "H.E.L.P." The letters stood for Helping, Encouraging, Loving and Providing, which we believed were the actions most needed in our community. H.E.L.P. Inc. was established by the ministerial Association and I was named as the first president. The organization has continued to grow and eventually moved into its own building.

In 2008, I was invited to return to Sandusky to speak at the 25th anniversary of H.E.L.P. The ministry continues to touch the lives of many people in the surrounding area.

Pastor Del finished his Bachelor degree at Spring Arbor College in 1984, and left Countryside to attend Asbury Theological Seminary. His ministry is fondly remembered by the Countryside folks and we remain close friends to this day.

In 1986, as I began of my seventh year at Countryside, I ask God to show me His will for my future. I sensed that God was doing something different in my life. It was clear that it was time to leave Countryside but I did not feel I was to go to another church as pastor. Through prayer, I believed that God was calling me to return to the ministry of evangelism which I had been involved in during college. This would be a great step of faith.

My biggest question as I thought about fulltime evangelism was where my family was going to live. I began to pray and waited to see how God would answer my prayer for a home. It was not long before the answer came. God provided an affordable home in Sandusky and paved the way for a new path of ministry for me. My years at Countryside had come to an end.

CHAPTER 17

Mama We Love You

The fall of 1987 brought a new sadness to my life. My mother died on Thanksgiving Day. Mama had been sick with cancer for over eight years. Chemotherapy, surgery and pain had been constant reminders of the disease that ate away at her body and caused her to look years older than she actually was.

There was a time, as this book tells, when I hated Mama. That all changed on February 6, 1965. When I gave my life to Christ, He gave me a new heart and my bitterness toward Mama was changed to love and concern for her salvation. After Julie and Eddie were saved, we all joined in prayer that God's love would save Mama from her sins.

The summer of 1965, Mom and Pop took us to see Mama while we were vacationing in Arkansas. We had a good visit but there was no opportunity to witness as I wanted to. Upon my return home to Michigan, Mama and I began to write to each other. I shared by letter what Christ had done in my life and told Mama I loved her and was praying for her. Our correspondence continued through my high school years, but I never talked to Mama face to face about Christ until the summer of 1971. Shortly after my final exams in my sophomore year at Asbury College, I drove to Arkansas to see Mama.

Mama was living in Newark, Arkansas with my father's half-brother, Walter Phillips. They had gotten together just a few months after Eddie and I moved to Michigan. Uncle Walter was good to Mama and had a stabilizing effect on her life. They were together for over 20 years. I had never met Uncle Walter and I knew almost nothing about him. I learned that my uncle was what I would call, "a good ole boy." He always made me feel at home.

Mama's new partner was far from wealthy. Some papers we found after his death revealed that in forty years he had a total income of just over $20,000. Although he was not rich, Uncle Walter was content to live in the kind of houses Mama was used to.

Arriving in Newark, I searched for the house Mama had described in her letters. Newark was a small town, just ten miles from Newport, where Julie, Eddie and I were born. Upon finding Mama and Walter's house, I found there was no running water or indoor bathroom, and the wiring was very bad. Two bare wires that hung from the living room ceiling powered every appliance and light in the house. Not only was the house a wreck, but their car was a piece of junk.

In spite of their meager possessions, they were very content. Uncle Walter took me to the backyard to show me the most beautiful garden I'd ever seen. My new stepfather loved to fish, garden and cut wood for his stove. I used to tease him that he was a "mountain man."

Uncle Walter was such a mountain man that the big city of Newark, population 600, began to cramp his style. As a result, he and Mama moved about two miles out of town.

It was during that first visit in Newark that Mama prayed and asked Jesus to come into her life. That was the beginning of Mama's Christian life, and through the years I watched her grow in her faith. For the next several years I kept in close contact with Mama by mail and traveled to see her whenever possible.

Mama tried to make up for all the bad times when drugs and alcohol ruled her life. She asked for forgiveness many times during those years and went out of her way to show her love. Once when my family and I were visiting, Mama insisted on paying for all meals when we ate out. My wife later commented that Mama was trying so hard to make up for the past. I assured Mama many times that the past was forgiven and she shouldn't worry about it.

In 1979, I received word that Mama had cancer that would eventually take her life. Mama wrote to Julie, Eddie and me, giving us the sad news. After Mama's death I found a letter that Julie sent to Mama after she received the news of Mama's cancer. The letter included the following:

Dear Mama,

I got your letter today and I haven't quit crying since. I am so sorry that something like this had to happen to you. I love you very much and I wish I could be there with you through this ordeal.

Mama, please remember that we all love you. Everyone wishes they had done things differently but there's no turning the clock back. The past is gone and forgotten so let's live now and have a good future. You could have beaten me daily and I would still love you, so forget about that. I'm proud you're my mother. I think we could have been real close if there hadn't been so many obstacles in the way. I understand now that you were so young to be a widow. I would be terrified in the same situation and I'm a lot older than you were. It must have been hard. You've suffered more than you deserve. You should be in for some blue skies now. So keep your chin up and remember we are praying for you. Remember, Mama, I love you and if you need something, let me know. I'll help you all I can.

Love always, Julie

Mama was to suffer for over 8 years before the cancer would take her life. During that time Uncle Walter took care of her like a father. We were so thankful that Uncle Walter was there through this difficult time.

In the summer of 1985, I decided to drive to Arkansas to see Mama. I invited Eddie and Pop to go with me and they both agreed. Pop, Uncle Walter's half-brother, had not seen his "mountain man" relative in years. During our visit the two of them spent a lot of time catching up on family events.

One of the funniest events of that visit took place one day as we stopped at the old house for a visit. Mama was sick and did not get out of bed, so we gathered in the bedroom so she could visit with us. It was very hot in the house and we each sought to find a cool place to sit. Uncle Walter smoked cigarettes that he rolled himself and as a result, the burning tobacco was constantly falling from the cigarette tip. As we found our places in the bedroom, Eddie sat in a chair in the corner. Uncle Walter took a chair between Eddie and a large fan blowing full blast toward Eddie. Every time a burning ember fell from Uncle Walter's cigarette, it would blow toward Eddie. Pop and I sat across the room and chuckled as Uncle Walter told his stories, and Eddie put out tiny fires that periodically hit his shirt. When our visit was over, Eddie emerged into the sunlight to find little holes burned all over the front of his shirt. Pop and I offered to take him to a burn unit for treatment but he refused. The next day we returned for another visit but Eddie grabbed Uncle Walter's chair and Uncle Walter sat in the corner burning holes in his own shirt.

In November of 1985, Julie called to tell me that Uncle Walter had died very suddenly of a heart attack. The graveside service was scheduled for 9 a.m. the very next morning. There was no way for me to get there in time for the service. Julie and I decided that she would go to the funeral and I would wait and go down later. We knew that Mama could not live alone as sick as she was. Julie took a late flight from San Antonio, Texas, to Little Rock, Arkansas, where her mother-in-law lived. Julie borrowed her car and drove to Newport, arriving just one hour before the service.

I called Mama the next two nights at her sister's motel. It was my desire to assure her of my love and prayers. During our conversations I told her that all she had to do was call and we would be there to help her. I began to pray that God would help me to know when to go to Arkansas and how to help when the time came. God answered my prayers in a marvelous way.

On the Friday before Thanksgiving Day 1986, Julie called to tell me she'd had several calls from Newark that Mama was terribly depressed and very sick. I told Julie I would leave for Arkansas on Monday morning.

That Friday afternoon I called the Department of Human Services in Batesville, Arkansas, to get some information concerning help for Mama. I knew I would not arrive in Arkansas until Tuesday and Thanksgiving Day was Thursday. This meant that I had Tuesday and Wednesday to secure help and housing for Mama before everything closed for the Thanksgiving holiday weekend. I had prayed but the time seemed so short.

The receptionist at the Department of Human Services connected me with a lady by the name of Myrtle Dugger. When I told Mrs. Dugger about Mama's situation, she told me that she knew Mama. She informed me that she had owned the grocery store in Newark where Mama and Uncle Walter lived. She shared some ideas with me and I thanked her for her help. I praised God for this small miracle, not realizing it was the beginning of a much larger miracle.

Following our conversation, Mrs. Dugger went into another room and shared our conversation with some co-workers. One of those co-workers was my cousin Patricia Gilmore. Patsy, as we always called her, was my Uncle Steve's granddaughter and had lived in the little apartment with us after our house burned. I had not seen Patsy since I left Mama on my thirteenth birthday in 1963. She later told me that she thought Mama was dead and had no idea what happened to Eddie and me.

Unaware of my cousin's discovery, my daughter Sarah and I left our home in Sandusky, Michigan, on Monday morning for Arkansas. Just one hour after our departure, Patsy called and spoke to my wife. She told her that I was on my way to Arkansas to find Mama a new place to live. My cousin began immediately to search for a nice place where Mama could live on her limited income.

Sarah and I arrived in Newport at 2 a.m. Tuesday morning. We went immediately to my aunt's motel, where a room awaited us. At 7 a.m. the phone began to ring. I was so sleepy I wasn't sure where I was when I picked up the receiver. When Patsy told me who I was speaking to, I could hardly believe my ears. After a few minutes of getting reacquainted, Patsy told me that she'd found a new home for Mama. We agreed to meet in Newark at 10 a.m. to visit the new accommodations.

I was so excited about what was happening that I got up, showered and woke Sarah up. Although we'd driven eighteen hours and only had five hours sleep, I wanted to see Mama and tell her the good news. My biggest concern at this point was whether Mama would be willing to leave the old house where she and Uncle Walter had lived for years.

Arriving at Mama's house, I began to call to her as soon as I got out of the car. By the time we got to her door Mama had poked her head out and I saw a big smile break across her face. Sarah and I were welcomed with hugs and kisses as we entered the dilapidated house. Looking around the house, I could see why Mama was so depressed. A long board stood in the kitchen to keep the ceiling from falling down. There was no running water and no bathroom in the house. Near the door a wood burning stove radiated heat. Mama had piled wood inches from the stove. I breathed a praise that the house had not caught fire.

The three of us sat down to visit and Mama began to cry. As I held Mama, she reminded me of a lost little girl, not knowing where to go or what to do. As she cried she kept telling me she thought she was going to die in the old house. I told Mama about my call from Patsy and the new home she'd found for her. Mama's tears turned to excitement at the prospect of her new home.

Patsy and I met at our appointed time in Newark and spent some time sharing the events of the almost twenty-five years we'd been separated. We drove back to Mama's and after a brief time of reunion, Patsy told us what she'd found. The Independence County Department of Human Services had purchased a large motel in Batesville and converted it into a home for adults on limited income. The residents of the Independence Inn had to be able to care for themselves but many services were provided. Mama wanted to see this place as soon as possible, so we left immediately for Batesville.

Arriving at the Inn, I could see a nice swimming pool, restaurant and beautiful grounds. We learned that each room had a private bath with running water, telephone and a television. We went to the manager's office and were given totals of cost, rules and services. After asking several questions, Mama asked when she could move in. "How about tomorrow morning?" the manager smilingly replied. Mama began to cry again. She was so happy that she almost forgot to ask where she was going to live.

The manager led us to the second floor and showed us two rooms. Both were very nice, overlooking the swimming pool. Mama wanted me to choose which room she should take. I chose the room with the brightest paint, for I felt that this would help Mama when she was depressed.

Returning to the parking lot, Patsy invited Mama, Sarah and me to her house for a catfish supper. As tired as I was, I just could not refuse catfish, so we followed Patsy home. Following supper Patsy shared about her life. Shortly after I left Mama in 1963, she was placed in a school for delinquent girls. Later, she was placed in a foster home with a Christian family. Patsy was now a Christian, a member of the Church of Christ and a social worker. As I listened, my heart was filled with praise for what God had done for us.

Mama was very tired so we cut our visit short and headed back to Newark, where Mama would spend her last night in the old house. The old house was cold when we arrived, because the wood stove had gone out. Mama put some pieces of wood in the stove, poured some diesel fuel on the wood and threw in a match. When the match hit the fuel, there was a small explosion. The stove literally jumped off the floor and the flames shot toward the ceiling. I closed the top of the stove but the flames were going up the chimney and shooting outside. I was afraid the house was going to catch fire but after a few minutes, the fire was under control. Not wanting to leave Mama alone in the house, I pleaded with her to go back to Newport with us but she insisted on staying at the house.

Sarah and I returned to the motel for some much needed rest. Bright and early the next morning we headed back to Mama's. I breathed a sigh of relief when the old house came into sight for I knew it had survived the night. Mama had her clothes and possessions packed and ready to move.

Before we packed the car for our trip to the Independence Inn, I had to go into Newark and take care of some business. The Independence Inn told us that we needed $300 to officially check Mama in. She had no money, so we decided we would sell the wood stove, her refrigerator and anything else she did not need.

I was very disappointed when I found that I could only get $30 for the wood stove, which was only two months old. The refrigerator, which was three months old, went to the highest bidder for $100. After I paid bills at the two grocery stores in town, I returned to let Mama know I had less than $10. At least Mama could leave town not owing a penny to anyone.

We packed the car with all of Mama's worldly goods. We had no trouble getting everything in the trunk of my car. No one could accuse Mama of worshipping material possessions.

Pulling away from the old house, I breathed a prayer that God would provide the $300 we needed to check Mama into her new home. As we drove through Newark, we stopped at the post office to fill out a change of address card. When asking if there was any mail, Mama was handed two letters. She opened them in the car and each had a check for $150. Two of Mama's sisters had sent the exact amount of money we needed. God had answered our prayer before we knew we needed it!

My heart was filled with praise as I watched Mama place her clothes in her closet and dresser drawers. She was like a little girl in a candy store as she arranged her meager possessions on her shelves and countertops.

Finishing the unpacking, we went to a nearby restaurant for a meal of celebration. On the way back to the Independence Inn, we stopped at a department store where I bought Mama a small plastic Christmas tree for her room. After decorating the little tree, Sarah and I returned to Newport; the date was November 26, 1986.

I decided to stop and visit my stepfather, Ed Eich. As we drove into the driveway of the gas station where he was working, I could see him under the hood of a car. Approaching the car he was working on, it felt good to see the man I once called Big Ed. When he saw us he stood up, smiled and started toward us. He looked much the same as I remembered when we lived together years before. Pleasant words were exchanged about our present lives and I gave him a report about Mama. He always asked about her and I was glad to learn he and Mama had become friends again.

The next day was Thanksgiving Day and Mama had asked Sarah and me to have dinner with her at the Independence Inn. Upon arriving we went to Mama's room where she was anxiously waiting for us. We had a wonderful Thanksgiving meal together. Several of the people living at the Inn came over and introduced themselves to Mama and welcomed her. It was the first Thanksgiving Day I had spent with Mama in twenty-four years.

That night, Sarah and I said goodbye and drove back to our motel. At 2 a.m. Friday morning I woke up and decided to head for home. By 2:30 a.m. Sarah and I were on the road. Driving out of Arkansas, I was thrilled with how God had answered my prayers for Mama. I kept thinking of how good He is to His children.

Sarah and I arrived home around noon the next day, after driving all night. I called Mama to let her know we'd arrived safely. It was the first time I had ever called my mother on the phone, as she had never had a telephone before. Mama said she was lonely but also expressed a great relief that she had a warm and safe place to live.

In the following weeks Mama and I talked many times on the phone. Each time I called, I found that she was feeling more at home. After a while she told me of several new friends she'd made.

Julie, Eddie and I began making plans to meet in Arkansas for a little family reunion. We decided to meet at Mama's new home in June of 1987. I was speaking in Denver, Colorado, and flew to Arkansas on my way home. Julie and her family drove from San Antonio, Texas, and picked me up at the Little Rock airport. We traveled together the rest of the way. Eddie was preaching in Oklahoma and drove to Arkansas on his way back to Michigan.

Julie and I arrived at the Independence Inn on Monday June 29th. Mama was waiting in her window as we drove into the parking lot. I left the others and headed for Mama's room. I got to the second floor just as Mama was coming out her door. When we met, we hugged and I picked Mama up and whirled her around. We went downstairs to meet the others. We went to lunch and had a nice meal and visit.

Eddie arrived the next day and the four of us had two days together. Mama and I took a trip to the cemetery in Newark where Uncle Walter was buried. It was the first time she had been there since the funeral. We then drove by her old house on our way to Newport. While we were in Newport we stopped by the garage where my stepdad worked. We had a good visit with him and then drove to the cemetery where Daddy was buried. Mama had not been to the Battle Axe cemetery, where her parents and several brothers and sisters were buried, for years. We shared many memories as we drove by the old Langston farm location just a mile away.

The next day Patsy invited all of us over to her house for a cookout. We visited, took pictures and ate some good food as the hours flew by.

When we got back to the Inn, Mama went to her room. Katherine, a lady who worked at the Inn, asked if she could speak to me. We went to her office and she told me that Mama was much sicker then she was letting us know. She shared that she didn't believe Mama would live long. I talked to Mama about this but she insisted that she was fine. It turned out that Katherine was right. Mama did not live long and this would be the last time I would be with her, this side of heaven.

The time went fast and soon it was time to say goodbye and head back for our separate homes and ministries. The next few months passed quickly and were very busy. My family moved into a new house. I entered full-time evangelistic work and had traveled to several states and Canada. Through all this activity, Mama and I kept in contact through mail and by phone.

Early in November of 1987, I received a call from the Independence Inn that Mama was very sick and was in the Newport Hospital. When I called the hospital, I was informed that Mama had had a chemotherapy treatment and later developed pneumonia. The nurse I spoke to said that Mama was getting better and that I should not worry. After two weeks, Mama went home to the Inn but within a week was seriously ill again. Her doctor had her put back into the hospital. I called her the first night after she was readmitted and Mama tried to assure me she would be all right.

When I called back two days later, the hospital informed me that Mama had checked out. I asked the nurse why Mama was sent home. The nurse informed me that she had left against their advice. I called Mama and she told me her bills were so big she couldn't afford to stay in the hospital. I later learned that Mama had thousands of dollars of bills she could not pay. I tried to persuade Mama to go back to the hospital and not worry about the bills, but she would not do it. I wonder now if Mama knew that she was dying and wanted to die in her own little room.

I kept in touch with the staff at the Inn and was working with them to find a nurse to come and take care of Mama. The people were so good to her there. They took turns taking her meals to her room and sitting with her. Patsy was also visiting Mama almost every day to check on her.

On Wednesday, November 25, 1987, I spoke to Mama for the last time. It was the day before Thanksgiving Day and I was very concerned about her. After the phone rang many times, she finally picked up the receiver. Her voice was so weak I could hardly hear her. She also had trouble staying awake as we spoke. I only kept her on the phone a few minutes and closed the conversation by saying, "Mama I love you." She told me she loved me too and hung up. I sat for a long time just holding the phone and thinking that I'd never talk to Mama again.

The following day we drove to Flint where we had Thanksgiving dinner. Mom, Pop, Eddie, Donny and Ned, Donny's older brother, and our families were all there. We had a nice meal, played some games and did a lot of laughing together. Eddie invited us to stop by his house on our way home.

As we sat visiting at Eddie's, the phone rang. Pop was calling to let us know that Julie had called him, trying to locate Eddie and me. Word had reached her from the Independence Inn that Mama had died that morning.

I knew it was coming but you are never totally prepared when the word finally comes. I cried when I heard that Mama was gone. The tears I shed were not for Mama, for I knew that she was so much better off with the Lord. I could not wish her back if I had the power. She was now in a place where there is no sorrow, pain, or tears.

Driving home, my mind went back to Thanksgiving Day the year before when Sarah and I were with Mama. I rejoiced that in the last year of her life Mama had a warm, safe and loving place to live. Mama had lived at the Independence Inn exactly one year to the day. I silently praised the Lord, through tears, for His answers to prayer and demonstration of love for Mama.

The following Sunday, Julie, Eddie and I were in Newport with our families for visitation at the funeral home. The funeral service was scheduled for Monday morning with Eddie doing all the scripture reading, Julie's husband, Donald, praying all the prayers and myself giving the message.

As we gathered for the service Monday morning, I was glad to see all the people who came. My stepfather attended the service and served as a pallbearer. My cousin Patsy was there, giving encouragement in her own special way. Several people from the Independence Inn came in a van driven by the manager. My cousin, Ray Langston, also came to the service. I had only seen him a couple of times in twenty-four years.

Just as the service started, I saw Mr. and Mrs. Ransom Smith slip into the chapel. Mrs. Smith had been my sixth-grade teacher and a wonderful Christian lady. She had paid for many of my school lunches during those terrible junkyard days. I was sitting in a restaurant earlier that very morning when Mrs. Smith came to my table and asked if I was Hal. I knew her immediately and we had a wonderful reunion. When she and her husband learned of the funeral, they rushed home, changed clothes and came to the service. Of all the teachers I have ever had, Mrs. Smith has always been my favorite. I was so thrilled that she could come to Mama's funeral.

The service went very well and I made it through the message before I broke down and began to cry. Just before the casket was closed, Mama's children and grandchildren stood at the casket, joined hands and wept together. The last words I spoke before the casket was closed were, "Mama, we love you." These were also the last words I said to Mama in our last telephone conversation and summed up the way we all felt. We buried Mama in the Battle Axe Cemetery next to Daddy and her two baby girls. It seemed so right for this to be her final resting-place.

We left Arkansas a few hours later and headed back to Michigan. During the long hours of driving I kept reflecting on all that God had done for my family. Mama was in heaven, her three living children were in full-time ministry, and so much bitterness and hate had been taken away by the wonderful love and grace of God.

If you don't know the Savior, why don't you do what we did? Ask Jesus to come into your heart, forgive your sins and give you eternal life. Then live for Him with all your strength. You will find out how wonderful He is and how good life can be. If I can help, please contact me and I will assist you in your new walk with Christ.

CHAPTER 18

Back On the Road

During my last year as pastor of the Countryside Church, I spent much time in thought and prayer about the new call I felt God had given me. I prayed that if this was God's will He would provide me a house for my family, as we had lived in church parsonages for 16 years. God did provide a house but it needed much work before I felt my family could move in. I used every spare hour over the next several months to do work on the house.

I had discovered the house through a real estate agent related to our church family. When I was first shown the house the sale price was $42,000. I considered putting in a bid but I felt checked because of the amount of work the house needed. I continued to pray and a few weeks later, the answer to my prayer came to pass. I received a call from the agent who informed me that the house was put on a special sale by F.H.A. for two days. If I wanted the house I could buy it for half-price at $21,000.

I immediately called my bank and inquired about a loan. I had never taken out a mortgage and I was not certain how the process worked. With the help of the mortgage officer, I filled out the application and submitted it to the bank. Within two weeks the loan was approved and I was a homeowner in answer to my prayers.

After the closing, I began to work on the house. With help from one of the church members, the plumbing in the kitchen and bathroom was completely replaced and the main floor was inhabitable. A couple from the community needed a place to live and I was able to rent the first floor of the house to them. I was sure that they would take good care of the house and they allowed me to come in and work on the upstairs whenever I wanted. The agreement was mutually beneficial.

I finished the painting and construction of two bedrooms in what had been an open attic. My daughter Sarah and son Stephen loved their new bedrooms. Although the rooms were not as big as the kids had had at the Countryside parsonage, they felt the rooms were theirs. I had a skylight put in when the roof was replaced. The skylight was half in Sarah's room and half in Stephen's room. They loved this as it added much needed light to the rooms and would open to allow proper ventilation.

At the end of July 1987, we had a very nice farewell party at the church and shortly thereafter we moved into our little house. It was not long before I was traveling and preaching again all over the United States in churches of several denominations. I was excited but at the same time, I dreaded being away from my children.

When I began my evangelistic ministry, I was booked for the remainder of 1987, and as I went through the fall of that year more invitations began to come. Before I finished my first year as a full time evangelist, I was booked for the second year and by the end of the second year, I was booked two years ahead. God had truly blessed me and the ministry He had led to me to follow.

There were two major problems that I faced as a full time evangelist. The first was being away from my two children. I would usually leave home on a Thursday and preach at a church Thursday night through Sunday night. As soon as the Sunday night service was over, I would head home and try my best to be home when Sarah and Stephen got up for school on Monday morning. I would take them to McDonalds for breakfast and then take them to school. This was very important to me.

One year Stephen was on a basketball team that played on Saturday mornings. Their coach had to quit because of some emergency situation and the team was going to dissolve if they did not find a new coach. I volunteered to be the new coach, even though I was on the road almost every weekend. During those weeks I would leave the church where I was preaching on Friday nights following the services. I would drive, sometimes all night, to get home. I would coach the basketball team on Saturday morning and then drive back to the church to preach Saturday night and Sunday before returning home on Sunday night. It was hard but it was worth it be with my son and serve as his coach.

I would also drive home on Friday nights to attend Sarah's basketball games. Sarah had a good coach but it was important to me to be there to show my support. I still have very fond memories of Sarah's basketball games. She was a good player and I was so proud to be her Dad watching and cheering from the bleachers.

The second major problem I faced as a fulltime evangelist was financial. I have never set a fee for preaching, sharing my testimony, or performing weddings and funerals. I also have never set a price for any of the ministry materials such as my books or recordings. I also did not believe is sending letters asking for financial donations. This sometimes put me in a tight financial situation and I prayed for guidance to help balance the books.

God showed me that I needed to work other jobs to make ends meet. After I took the kids to school on Monday morning, I would go to work at the Buyers Guide, a local shopper magazine. I spent one day a week taking care of their Accounts Receivable department. This often took me to small claims' court where I would do as many as twenty cases in a single day. I learned a great deal working this part time job.

God also led me to undertake a new ministry in Christian counseling and I began the New Creation Christian Counseling Center. I had a Master's Degree in Christian counseling and was a Registered Social Worker with the State of Michigan. At one time I had an office at home, in the Buyers Guide building after office hours and an office in Lapeer, Michigan.

I counseled with dozens of individuals and couples and never once did I ever charge a fee. If folks wanted to make a donation to my ministry, it was deeply appreciated. One time I remember a lady coming for counseling who had no money. I worked with her for several months and one night she came for her counseling session with a large plastic bag. She apologized for not being able to donate financially and then presented me with a dressed turkey from her farm. It reminded me of an episode of "Little House on the Prairie" where folks brought such gifts to the doctor for medical services. I still remember the "turkey payment" with great fondness.

During my time as a fulltime evangelist, I also continued teaching a class called "Biblical Perspectives" for Spring Arbor College. I taught the class one night a week for five weeks and the income I received helped pay the bills. I taught for Spring Arbor College the entire time I was doing evangelistic work.

For three years I traveled thousands of miles preaching in churches, camps, schools, once in a movie theater and in a two car garage converted into a sanctuary. The evangelistic ministry was going well but things at home were beginning to fall apart. At the end of my third year on the road, Sarah and Stephen came to me with a plea to come off the road and be home more.

I could see this as the beginning of the end of my evangelistic ministry but at that time, I did not realize that this was the beginning of the end of life as I had known it for almost twenty years. I was about to enter the most traumatic time in my life since 1963 when I said goodbye to my mother on my thirteenth birthday. How was I going to survive what was coming next?

CHAPTER 19

It All Crashes Down

Because of problems at home, my children, Sarah and Stephen, came to me and pleaded with me to leave the road and the evangelistic ministry. I began to pray for God's guidance in this present situation. It was not long before things began to rapidly change.

Before one of my revival meetings in the fall of 1991, I received a phone call from Pastor Wayne Schreffler. He was pastor of a Free Methodist Church in New Castle, Pennsylvania. I had preached one revival meeting at this church the year before. Pastor Schreffler informed me that his wife, Bobbi was in the hospital following a serious stroke. She was in intensive care and the pastor did not think there was any way she could be home by the time of the revival meeting.

We made the decision to not cancel the revival and agreed to pray together that God would somehow use this illness for His glory. I was concerned about Bobbi and began to ask everyone I knew to pray for her healing. She was a great woman of prayer herself, and I prayed that God would be gracious and bring healing to her body.

When I arrived at the church parsonage in New Castle, I was greeted by Mrs. Bobbi Schreffler. I was surprised by her presence as she greeted me with smiles and hugs. Bobbi asked me to come in and sit down so she could tell me about her miracle of healing.

Bobbi shared with me that she was in intensive care and paralyzed on her right side when God answered our prayers. She told me that Jesus came into the room and began to sing her a song. At first she thought she might be dying, but following Jesus' song, Bobbi realized she was no longer paralyzed. She called the nurses who in turn called the doctors. After a thorough examination there was no evidence that Bobbi had even had a stroke. She was released the next day and returned to her daily activities.

When Bobbi told me about her experience of Jesus singing her a song, I remembered my experience a few years before when I heard a song in the sanctuary at Countryside Church. I shared my "song experience" for the first time with the Schrefflers and we were amazed at how similar our miracles were. Since that time I have shared my miracle, of Jesus or an angel singing me a song, with many people.

I needed that experience with the Schrefflers as I was entering a very difficult time in my life and ministry. My marriage was about to end and I needed to know that Jesus was by my side. Through those very difficult days, Jesus never left my side. As I look back, I can see so clearly His working in my life.

I cannot go into details here about all that happened, but I assure you everything humanly possible was done to save the marriage. Divorce was something I never wanted and prayed would never happen. As I now look back after over 23 years, I can honestly say, that in the same situation, the outcome would be the same. If I could have found another way, I promise you, I would have taken it.

God directed me to resign as an evangelist, cancel my revival schedule, turn in my ministerial credentials and seek a full time job at the Buyers Guide. I had worked there one day a week for the past three years. Then just when I needed it, God opened the doors for a full time position. All of this happened within one week.

For the first time since the Asbury Revival in 1970, I had nowhere to preach and was no longer an evangelist or a pastor. This was such a strange experience. I truly believed that my life as a minister was over but my faith in the Lord remained strong.

God had already seen me through so many difficult crises in my life. I believed that God would show me the way through this crisis as well. I just had to keep my eyes on Jesus and let Him carry me when I could not go on.

As I was beginning this new phase in my life I had hoped that the toughest time was behind me. I was wrong, as I would soon learn of one more heartache I had to face before that year was over.

Early on Christmas morning 1991, the kids and I opened our presents and for a little while things seemed happy. My good friends, Harry and Ruthann Walker, brought us Christmas dinner, as I could not cook a decent meal. Sarah, Stephen, and I were enjoying our meal when the phone rang.

As I answered the phone, I could hear someone screaming but I could not understand what they were saying. After a few moments, I realized it was my brother, Don, and he was crying, "Pop is dead, Pop is dead." Pop did not show up at Don's house for Christmas dinner, so he sent his wife Beth to check on him. She found Pop dead in his home.

Pop had battled heart disease for many years. He had his first heart attack when I was still in high school and had had two open heart surgeries. Pop was just 62 years old when he died. He had been my confidant during this recent difficult time and had encouraged me in my decisions. I truly felt more alone in my present crisis as I had not shared a lot of information with other family members.

I did not tell the kids of Pop's passing until the next day. I controlled my emotions until they went to bed that evening. I did not want any more sadness for them than they had already experienced on that Christmas Day.

As I sat in the living room after Sarah and Stephen were asleep, I cried out to God. I asked God to please give me a Word of hope in this time of terrible heartache. I opened my Bible and began to read and God answered my prayer in a matter of minutes. I turned to the book of Joel in the Old Testament and as I came to Joel 2:25-26, it was as if the Words of hope jumped off the page.

In Joel 2:25-26 God promises Israel, "I will give you back what you lost to the swarming locust, the hopping locusts, the stripping locusts, and the cutting locusts... Once again you will have all the food you want, and you will praise the Lord your God, who does these miracles for you. Never again will you be disgraced." I clung to these Words of hope and restoration as I faced the difficult years ahead.

As I look back over these many years, I can see so clearly how the promises in these verses have been fulfilled in my life. God is faithful to be with us and to see us through the most difficult situations. No matter what trial we may have, God will make something beautiful of our ashes if we remain faithful to Him.

CHAPTER 20

Rebuilding My Life

Following the events of December 1991, my marriage ending, Pop dying, and losing my ministry, I began to try to bring some sense of normal living back to our home. I had conducted Pop's funeral between Christmas and New Year's Day and continued working for the Buyer's Guide to try to make ends meet financially. If it were not for my pension funds that were available, I would have had to file bankruptcy. God again provided a way to move forward.

One day I was looking through some books I had kept from my library. I came across a book that I had owned for several years. The book was entitled, "Rebuilding Your Life" by Dr. Dale Gallaway. The book was written by a pastor who had lost his family and his ministry and had to rebuild his life from nothing. The story was very inspiring. Dr. Gallaway told how God directed him in "how to survive depression and a sense of hopelessness" and find a new happiness and a greater ministry than he had ever known. He later became a professor of pastoral ministries at Asbury Theological Seminary where I had been accepted years before.

After reading how God restored and blessed Dr. Gallaway, I was determined to be faithful to God with all my heart. I could only hope and pray that God would restore me to ministry. I remembered a small cross someone in a revival meeting in Grayling, Michigan had given me a few years before. On the little stained glass cross were the words, "With God, all things are possible." I believed those words and prayed each day that God would work a miracle for me and my children.

My highest priority during those difficult days was to find a church home for myself and my children. I felt strongly that I should get out of town and make a fresh start with a new church family. I had preached a revival the year before at a small country Bible Church about 20 miles from my home. I spoke with my kids and we all agreed to give the little church a try.

For the next year, I attended that little country church. I was there for Sunday School, morning worship, Sunday evening services and Wednesday night Bible study. I have loved going to church since becoming a Christian in 1966. That desire did not wane when I was no longer a pastor. I found great strength in worshipping and studying with God's people.

During that year I did not lead worship or Bible studies. I felt the Lord was saying to me, "Be still and know that I am God." I waited for the Lord as I knew this would bring me strength as Isaiah 40:31 says, "They that wait upon the Lord will renew their strength, they will mount up with wings like eagles, they shall run and not be weary, they shall walk and not faint." I held onto that promise, and as always, God kept his Word. Each week I felt stronger, whatever adversity came my way.

While things were going well with our new church, things were tough at the Buyer's Guide. I was given every account that no other salesperson wanted. I had over 100 accounts and after calling on every one of those accounts, I did not sell one ad. I was very discouraged by this terrible failure at my new job.

I remember well the day I sat in my car, after another failure to sell an ad to a merchant, in the little town of Peck, Michigan. I began to cry and told the Lord that I could not do this job and I wanted to quit. Quitting was totally against what I had taught my kids. My rule was that you never quit a job unless you have another job lined up. I had no job to go to if I quit, but I did not know how long I could hold on to this job if I did not start selling advertising.

As I sat in the car crying and the rain began to fall, God spoke to me. It was as if Jesus came and sat in the car with me and softly said, "I am going to teach you something." I remembered Jeremiah 33:3 which says, "Call unto Me and I will show you great and mighty things that you do not know." My heart jumped with joy as I anticipated what God would teach me.

To make a long story short, within a year, I was referred to fondly by the staff at the Buyer's Guide as "Ad Man." Within two years I was promoted to sales developer and later I was offered the job of sales manager for the company. God had truly kept His promise, had taught me many things and had shown me success in a job where I did not want to be.

My heart was still yearning for ministry. The sales position just did not fulfill my heart's calling. Yet there were many times as a salesman that

I had opportunity to witness and minister to people. I met people with all kinds of problems and I was able to share the hope of Christ with them.

At the little Bible Church I made some wonderful friends and my kids made friends with other teenagers in the Sunday School and other church activities. Every week I would attend the Wednesday night Bible study and I always sat in the same seat. I think that was a part of being a Methodist for so many years.

Every Wednesday night I sat behind a lady who attended the Bible study faithfully. Her name was Kathy and she had two teenage children who just happened to be the same ages as my kids. We spoke often as the Bible study was dismissed and we waited for our kids to come from youth meeting. One week she invited me to come to her house to hear a presentation by her Amway group leader. I was hesitant as I had had very little social contact outside of church and family. I was not excited about meeting a bunch of strangers.

After thinking it over, I agreed to attend the Amway meeting. I was determined that I would never become an Amway guy. I felt I was doing all of the sales work I would ever want to do. I did not know at the time, but this Amway meeting would be a life changing meeting for me. God does work in mysterious ways.

The night of the Amway meeting, I arrived to the sound of laughter as smiling people surrounded me with hugs and greetings. The evening was a delight and I made friendships that night that are very precious to me to this day, over 20 years later. That night, to my surprise, I became an Amway guy.

The Amway group was made up of several folks and most of them were Christians. The small group that I joined was a part of a larger group that met periodically at Olivet Nazarene College in Kankakee, Illinois. The larger group in Illinois was strongly Christian and I found great fellowship with new brothers and sisters in Christ from all over the midwest. The rallies that we attended were almost like large revival meetings with inspiring speakers and great gospel music. I could not believe how much I felt at home with these wonderful folks.

With each of the trips to Illinois, I got to know my sponsor better and learned that her life situation was much like mine. Kathy told me of a husband who had left her and her children for another woman and how things had gone downhill over the years. More recently, she had been desperately hurt by the failure of a relationship with an abusive man. Kathy found herself and her kids living in a travel trailer at a Christian campground one summer and from there to a tent. She hit rock bottom when she could not enroll her kids in school because they did not have an address. They were considered homeless.

Kathy was a strong Christian and cried out to the Lord. As a result God provided her with a home for her and her kids as well as a job at a local grocery store. Her testimony was strong and I grew to highly respect her as a Christian. Kathy had much encouragement for me in my situation. The whole Amway thing was just what I needed at that time in my life.

The first weekend the group attended the Amway rally at Olivet Nazarene College. The rally lasted until late on Saturday night. The group usually headed home Sunday morning but I insisted that we needed to go to church. I found a church near the college that had an early service. We could attend the early service and then head home and still arrive home early Sunday evening. At the close of the service, the pastor gave an invitation to receive Christ and a young lady in our group responded and gave her life to Jesus. I was blessed when I arrived home. It was almost like the feeling of coming home from one of the revival meetings I had held over the years.

Once a year the Amway group traveled to a large national gathering where some top named groups sang and nationally known speakers shared their Amway success stories. I attended two of the large gatherings.

On the first trip, our group of five flew to Miami, Florida where we stayed at the Fontainbleau Hotel on Miami Beach. It was a beautiful place and I was excited to be in such a positive atmosphere.

When the room assignments were given, I was sure the other man in our group and I would be on the "street side" of the hotel. I thought I would probably end up sleeping on the floor as there were supposed to be four other men in our room. When we arrive at our room, we were delighted to find that we were on the "ocean side" of the hotel with a magnificent view. The other four men that were assigned to our room never showed up so I had my own huge bed. I felt like a king!

I found out later that day that the three ladies in our group ended up in a "street side" room with three other ladies. Kathy slept on the floor during the entire weekend. My buddy and I offered to trade rooms with the ladies but they declined. I felt a little guilty, but I still enjoyed the view very much. I returned from the rally refreshed and ready to sell a bunch of advertising but still my heart yearned for ministry.

Kathy knew I was not happy working at the Buyer's Guide and she would ask me periodically when I was going to ask God to restore my ministry. I did not want to get my hopes up to then be disappointed if it was not God's will. In private, I did often tell God if He would ever allow me to return to ministry as a pastor or evangelist, I would be so grateful.

After several months of doing nothing but sitting in church, the pastor asked me if I would counsel with an individual in the church. I was happy to speak with the person and found a great blessing in working with the person who was going through a time of severe trial. After that time of counseling, I sensed that God was nudging me towards doing more counseling.

I asked permission at the Buyer's Guide to use one of the offices during evening hours to do counseling and began to meet with folks needing Christian counseling. I had one person ask me how I could ever counsel with others when I could not even keep my own family together. I wanted to go into a lengthy explanation of all the events of the twenty year marriage, but decide it would make no difference. That person had made up their mind about me and I was not going to change their thinking.

One of the people who came to see me during that period of time was a man named Butch. He was going through a divorce and needed someone to talk to. As we talked over a period of several months, Butch and I became close friends. Our stories were very similar and we encouraged each other to keep the faith and never give up.

Kathy and I were becoming closer friends. One Sunday she invited me to her house for dinner later in the week. It was an interesting evening as her dog Angel tried to eat me for dinner. I truly thought the dog would kill me if she got through the storm door that separated us.

After Angel calmed down, I sat down to a delicious, very HOT, Mexican dinner. Kathy liked her food spicy but I have always been a wimp when it came to eating spicy food. As I sat with tears running down my cheeks, Kathy thought I was emotional because she had fixed me a nice dinner. When she realized that the tears were because of spice and not emotion, she apologized and got me some cold water. We still laugh about the first HOT dinner she made for me.

Following dinner that night, I told Kathy how God had given me a special promise in Joel 2 to restore the years the locust have devoured. With excitement Kathy shared how years before God had given her the same promise from the same passage in Joel. We sat in amazement that God had spoken to both of us from the same verses in God's Holy Word. It was the first time we had received the same message from God but it would not be the last time.

After a year at the little Bible Church, God began to speak to me about returning to ministry. I wanted to be sure, so I began to pray in earnest that God would open the doors for ministry, if this was His will.

It became very clear, very quickly, that God was leading me back to ministry but I was not sure of what to do. The denomination of the little

Bible Church would never let a divorced man be a minister. I knew if I was to follow God's leading, I would have to say goodbye to the little church and attend a church that would accept me into ministry.

The Free Methodist Church superintendent had attended Pop's funeral in December of 1991. He told me he would support me if I wanted to return to ministry in the Free Methodist Church. I prayed about returning to the Free Methodist Church and felt that was not the direction God wanted me to go. After much prayer seeking God's direction, I began to attend First United Methodist Church in Brown City, Michigan.

Before I left the little Bible Church I had lunch with the pastor and shared with him that I believed that God was leading me back into ministry. I also told him that I was leaving the church and seeking God's direction to return to ministry. I gave the pastor a farewell letter to be read to the congregation, thanking them for their love and support.

When I told Kathy of my plans, she smiled and said, "That's interesting." What was interesting was that God had been telling Kathy that she was to leave the Bible Church and take her kids to First United Methodist Church. First United Methodist Church had a large youth program and her children, Jason and Stephanie, had been attending their youth meetings for several months because several of their friends from school attended. She felt she should take her kids where they would enjoy church and youth group the most.

This was the second time when God spoke to both Kathy and I at the same time about the same matter. To me it was a sign that God had brought someone into my life who was truly close to God and could help me to be closer to God myself. The following Sunday, we walked into the First United Methodist Church with our four teenagers. A few heads turned but no one passed out and it was a very enjoyable service.

Pastor Jim Walker welcomed Kathy and me with open arms. As I shared over the next few weeks that I believed God was leading me back into ministry, the pastor assured me of his prayers and support. The first step towards becoming a minister in the United Methodist Church was to become a member of the local church. After attending the church for a month, Kathy and I became members of the First United Methodist Church. I was returning to the denomination where I had given my life to Christ in 1966.

One day I received a call from my friend Butch. Butch told me he was getting married and asked me if I would be the best man at his wedding. I was deeply honored and accepted his invitation. He also told me that he was marrying a lady who was a United Methodist minister. It seemed that

I was beginning to see God moving in one of His mysterious ways again and continued to pray for guidance.

Butch informed me during our conversation that he was no longer the same man he used to be and as a result, he was no longer Butch. His new name was Clarence, his given name. Butch had been a nickname for many years. Clarence was a new man in Christ and was beginning a new life with a wonderful Christian minister as his new wife.

Clarence married a beautiful Christian lady named Earlene. Earlene was the pastor of two United Methodist churches in the area. At Clarence and Earlene's wedding, I was introduced to Rev. Ken Towsley who was the United Methodist district superintendent in the area. I shared my interest in returning to ministry and ask him to please call me if I could be of service.

Rev. Towsley did not know me. I wondered if I would ever hear from him. I prayed again for God's will to be done and waited for doors to open in God's perfect timing. Rev. Towsley called me a month later. He asked if I was available to fill in for a part time pastor who had been kicked by one of his cows and was suffering from a broken hip.

I jumped at the opportunity to serve as a pastor. For the next six weeks as Pastor Pohly recovered from the accident I was able to preach and carry out pastoral duties. I asked Kathy if she would attend the church with me, as I really did not want to go by myself. She agreed and this experience turned out to be as great a blessing for Kathy as it was for me. The pastor's wife attended every service. She took Kathy under her wing with no judgment or condemnation as she shared many bits of wisdom that would prove to be very valuable in our future.

The folks at the church loved Kathy and me as if we were part of their family. They even asked if it might be possible for us to return to be their pastor when their pastor retired. I was very happy to hear their enthusiasm, but I knew it would be several years before their pastor retired as he was a man of incredible strength and resilience. I was convinced that God had opened this door to show the district superintendent that I could handle the responsibility of being a pastor.

After six weeks, the pastor returned to his pulpit and we said farewell to the wonderful church family. It was a sad parting, as I loved being their pastor. It caused me to have a greater yearning to return to pastoral ministry. Kathy reminded me that I was "called by God" and no man could stop what God had ordained. All I could do was to wait and pray.

I received a call from my good friend Clarence a few weeks later. He informed me that he and his new wife were going to be leaving the area and move to the upper peninsula of Michigan to make a fresh start. I knew that

Clarence loved to ride motorcycles and ask him how he would handle the very cold weather of upper Michigan. He assured me he would do just fine, then he surprised me with news of a request his wife Earlene had made.

Pastor Earlene had asked the district superintendent that I be her replacement at the two churches where she was pastor. I was blessed to know she had that kind of confidence in me and also sensed that God was at work in restoring me to ministry. Again I spent much time seeking God's guidance and wisdom concerning my future.

During this time of waiting to hear from the district superintendent, I spent time praying about another major decision in my future. I felt strongly that I was to ask Kathy to be my wife and partner as I returned to ministry. This decision made me more nervous than the prospect of being a pastor again.

After much thought and prayer, I asked Kathy to be my wife. I had purchased a ring that I was privileged of designing myself. I showed it to Kathy as I asked for her hand in marriage, but her response was less than enthusiastic. She just stared at me as if she was in shock. I knew that this great plan of mine was falling far short of my expectations.

I was disappointed that Kathy did not say, "Yes." I told Kathy that I wanted her to keep the ring and pray about my proposal and that I would accept whatever decision she made. A week later, I stopped by her house while running my sales route for the Buyer's Guide. As I sat down in her kitchen to visit for a few minutes, I noticed that she had the ring on her finger. I jumped up and with great excitement I hugged her. She then said, "Yes, I will marry you!" My heart leapt with joy. I was beginning to see everything coming together just as God had promised me on that Christmas day almost two years before.

The next step for me was to go to Kathy's parents and ask permission to marry their daughter. Kathy's parents, Pete and Donna Princing, were a wonderful, caring couple. They had accepted my friendship with Kathy and always treated me with love and kindness.

As we arrived at their home the day I was to ask for Kathy's hand in marriage, I thought my nose was beginning to run. When I wiped my hand across my face, I discovered it was covered with blood. I could not remember the last time I had had a nosebleed; I have not had another since then. I can only speculate that I was so nervous that my blood pressure shot up and thus the nosebleed. We still joke about it from time to time.

What a sight I must have been, standing at my fiancé's parent's door with tissues over my nose and blood all over my Michigan sweatshirt. After "Ma" helped to clean me up, I asked for Kathy's hand and her parents graciously agreed. As I sat in my blood stained sweatshirt, I silently praised

God for His leading and the hope of beginning a new life. We immediately began to make plans for a small family wedding.

Kathy and I were both working fulltime jobs and did not have much vacation time so we decided to get married on Thursday evening of Memorial Day weekend. By doing this, we could have a three day honeymoon and would not miss too much work.

On May 27, 1993, Kathy and I were married at the First United Methodist Church in Brown City, Michigan. Pastor Jim Walker officiated at the ceremony and all four of our children were in the wedding party. There were a "few" other folks at the wedding also, as Pastor Walker decided, without informing Kathy or me, to put our wedding in the church bulletin and invite the entire church to attend. We had planned a small wedding for just our families and a few friends. It turned out to be a great wedding with a large gathering of friends from all over the area.

As the ceremony concluded, I did something that I have never witnessed by a newly wedded husband. I began to cry. These were happy tears and they came so suddenly, I myself was taken by surprise. I hugged every person coming through the reception line and had to blow my nose a few time during the process. I could not remember a time when I was so happy. God was blessing me and beginning the restoration of my new life.

On May 27, 1993, Sarah, Stephen and I were given a wonderful new family. I received a loving wife and stepmother for my kids. Also, Sarah and Stephen received a new brother and sister, Jason and Stephanie. We knew there were going to be many adjustments in our lives but by God's grace and power we believed everything would work out for good.

The day Kathy and I got married we had four teenagers, two full time jobs and I was doing counseling part time. There were also two dogs and a guinea pig living at our new home. The task of bringing everyone together to form a unified family unit seemed overwhelming at times, but with God's help we did it.

A huge part of God's promise of restoring my life was fulfilled on May 27, 1993, but God was far from finished in restoring my life and all that I had lost. The next step in God's plan was coming soon and I waited with anticipation to see what blessing was coming next.

CHAPTER 21

Back To Ministry

Kathy and I took our honeymoon on Miami Beach. We could not afford to stay at the Fontainebleau Hotel so we got a less expensive motel that had a "small" view of the ocean. The big difference between this trip to Miami Beach and the trip we took with the Amway group was that we got to stay in the same room. We had a wonderful weekend. And then we flew home to undertake the many challenges of building a blended family, keeping our marriage strong and both working full-time jobs.

Just a week after returning from Miami, I received a phone call from Rev. Ken Towsley, the United Methodist Church district superintendent. I nervously listened as he asked if I would be interested in becoming the half time pastor of the Omard United Methodist Church of Brown City, Michigan and the Cole United Methodist Church of Yale, Michigan. These were the two churches where my friend Clarence's new wife, Earlene, was serving as pastor.

I immediately said, "Yes, I would love to be the pastor of the churches." I could not wait to tell Kathy of this new miracle of restoration that God had given us. She was excited but also a little apprehensive as she had never been a pastor's wife and everything was happening like a whirlwind. She was not sure she could fill the role "pastor's wife" adequately. My advice to her was, "Honey you take care of me and with the Lord's help I will take care of the churches." With a big hug and a prayer, we came up with a plan to tell our four teenagers that they were all going to be PKs (Preacher's Kids).

Jason, Sarah, Stephen and Stephanie accepted the news and our entire family waited for July 1st of 1993, when we would officially be assigned to the Omard and Cole Churches, as a half-time local pastor. I began to prepare an introductory sermon for the first Sunday. I wanted that day to be very special for everyone in our family and for the churches.

Our first Sunday at Omard and Cole was July 4, 1993. I guess the 4th of July fit pretty well as the new pastor and wife arrived as newlyweds with four teenagers. I am sure there were fireworks going off in the minds of some of the folks. It was not long until we felt at home with the folks from both of the churches and they felt at home with us. They became our new extended families.

For the next three years, Kathy sat on the front row of the Omard church at 11 a.m. with our four teenagers next to her. I will never forget preaching to our four kids, knowing they would be watching me all through the week to see if I really believed and lived what I was preaching.

As I look back, I really miss those days and wish I could go back and relive just one of those Sunday mornings at the Omard Church. Those were happy days filled with fond memories of my family together in God's house.

During my three years at Omard and Cole Churches, I was given the opportunity to become the sales manager at the Buyer's Guide. I had worked full time as a sales representative for two years when this new position opened up. There was only one requirement that I did not meet to receive the position. I was told that I must resign my two churches so I could put all of my energy towards sales. I refused to resign the churches and the company hired another person to become the sales manager. I was back in ministry and nothing was going to take me out again.

After that experience with the sales manager position, I decided that I was going to get out of the sales business. I began to look for opportunities to minister to people in some kind of counseling or care ministry. I discovered a position with a professional counseling center in Port Huron, Michigan. They were looking for a person to work with dysfunctional families and intervene before their children were taken away from the home by the state. I thought this was a good fit with my childhood, background and ministry. I applied for the job.

I was excited when I was called for an interview and then a second interview followed. A few days after the second interview, I received a call from the director of the counseling center. She informed me that I had been chosen for the position ahead of several other applicants. I could see this job as a perfect fit with what I was doing as a pastor. My thoughts were to resign from the Buyer's Guide to enter this new work while still serving half time as pastor of the Omard and Cole Churches.

That thought was dashed when the director informed me that to get the position, I would have to resign my two churches. The counseling center wanted me on call 24 hours a day and believed the churches would interfere with my availability to do my job. I immediately told the director that I would not resign the churches and if it meant losing the job, I would withdraw my name from consideration. The next day the counseling center hired another person to fill the position. I was again disappointed but determined to stay in ministry at all costs.

It was during my years at Omard and Cole Churches that Mom passed away. Mom had been in a nursing home for ten years, suffering from Alzheimer's disease. Pop had taken care of her at home as long as possible. When Mom began to get out of the house and walk away, he was forced to place her in a nursing home where she had 24 hour care. In the fall of 1994, I received word that Mom had been taken to the hospital after aspirating some food. Before we could get to the hospital we received word that Mom had gone to Heaven. She was 74 years old and had spent many of those years helping me to come to know Jesus and to grow in His love.

Don, Eddie and I officiated at Mom's funeral. My daughter, Sarah sang the beautiful song "Thank You" as we remembered the wonderful testimony of this great Christian lady. Her funeral was a celebration of a life well lived.

Only eternity will tell the influence that Mom's testimony had upon the world. Just in the lives of four of her sons is a total of over 100 years of ministry. I believe thousands of people can trace their spiritual heritage back to Mom. I was so blessed to have her influence in my life. Mom is now in Heaven receiving her reward for being a faithful child of God.

During the three years at Omard and Cole Churches, all four of our teenagers graduated from high school. Sarah and Stephen graduated from Sandusky High School where they had gone to school all their lives. Jason and Stephanie graduated from Brown City High School where they had attended for several years. All four of them were honored and given graduation Bibles in morning worship services at both Cole and Omard Churches.

Jason and Sarah graduated on the same day, at the same time, so Kathy and I had to go in different directions to graduations, which made us sad. Stephen and Stephanie graduated the same year but on different days, so we were able to attend both of their graduations, which made us very happy.

Remember I told you the Omard and Cole circuit was not a full time assignment. As much as we loved the folks at Omard and Cole, I knew if I was to ever reestablish my full ministerial credentials, I needed to be a full time pastor. I again began to ask God to open a door. This time I was praying God would open the door to full time ministry. God heard my prayers and He began to lead me towards my dream of full time ministry.

We had three good years of ministry at Omard that culminated on our last Sunday as we celebrated the Omard United Methodist Church's 100th anniversary. Kathy and I won the "centennial mini float" contest that last Sunday and I had my centennial beard shaved off as a part of the celebration. Leaving was bittersweet as we had grown to love the people, but God was leading us forward.

The Cole Church was also a wonderful church and had many wonderful folks who loved us and supported our ministry faithfully. They actually came with us in our next move to make a temporary, 3 church circuit.

Their beautiful building was only about ten years old and sat on top of a little hill with a circle drive. The first time I walked through the doors of the Cole Church, I told Kathy that the sanctuary seemed very familiar but I was not sure why. Several weeks later, I was approached by one of the members who ask if I remembered him. I told him I did remember him from the Sunday services. He then told me we had met in the 1980's, when I was the pastor of the Countryside Free Methodist Church in Sandusky, Michigan. The original Cole Church had been struck by lightning and burned. As the Cole Church was in the process of rebuilding, he visited the Countryside Church and thought it was very beautiful. He requested to borrow the Countryside building plans to study in preparation for building the new Cole Church. As this gentleman told me this story, I again breathed a prayer of thanksgiving as I could see again God's hand at work in restoring that which I had lost. I felt so at home in the Cole Church sanctuary because it reminded me so much of the Countryside Church sanctuary where Jesus or an angel had sung to me.

Another blessing I received at the Cole Church was meeting Hollis and Lisa Clark. Hollis was tall, strong and had shoulder length hair and a beard. He looked more like the pictures of Jesus I had seen than anyone I have ever met. Hollis and Lisa began to attend church regularly while we were at Cole and later Lisa received the call to ministry. We have remained close friends ever since.

With the many prayers Kathy and I had about a full time appointment, our answer finally came. The United Methodist Churches in Capac, Michigan were going through a very difficult time. Their pastor had been diagnosed with multiple sclerosis and had gone on disability leave. As a result, the Zion and First United Methodist Churches of Capac, which together formed the Capac circuit, were without a pastor. A retired pastor was providing pastoral leadership until July 1, 1996, when a new pastor would be appointed.

After praying about it with Kathy, I made a call to our new district superintendent Rev. Marvin McCallum. I asked him about the possibility of me being appointed to the Capac Churches. Rev. McCallum told me that it was possible but not likely because I was still in the process of restoring my ministerial credentials. The churches had always had full members of the conference as pastors, but Rev. McCallum promised that he would do his best. I was grateful for his help.

Within a few weeks, I received a call from Rev. McCallum informing me that our bishop had appointed me to the Capac Zion and First United Methodist Churches. The churches had a nice parsonage that was remodeled before we moved in. The folks from the church seemed very friendly and I had big dreams for my first full time appointment as a United Methodist pastor. God's timing is always perfect.

The appointment to Capac seemed perfect as the town was closer to Kathy's job as the office manager of a State Farm Insurance office in Lapeer, Michigan. I would no longer have to work selling advertising or need to do part time counseling. I was praising God as we made the move to the Capac parsonage and settled in to a regular schedule of pastoral responsibility. I was a full time pastor once again, we had a nice parsonage to live in and we were empty-nesters. God was good.

When we arrived in Capac, the average attendance of the Zion Church was 60 and the average attendance at First Church was 20. The church buildings were large enough to provide ministry to many more than the 80 people. I began to pray for guidance in how to grow the churches, to bring new people to Christ and to eternal life. This would prove to be more difficult than I ever imagined.

Before the end of my first year, a large group of people left the Zion Church in protest of my leadership style. It was shocking to see the congregation lose 20 of its regular attendees in one Sunday. This was the first time in my ministry that a group of people left a church I was serving as pastor. I cried out to the Lord and ask for guidance in how to deal with this new experience. I felt God assuring me that if I would be patient, I would see a miracle take place.

Before the group left we had many visitors attend the Zion Church but very few ever returned after their initial visit. You could feel tension in the services. I believe visitors could also sense it and did not come back. I shared with Kathy that preaching at the Zion Church was very difficult. As much as I enjoyed preaching, I almost dreaded preaching at Zion because I sensed so much resistance.

Following the exodus from the church, our church treasurer informed the administrative board that we were in financial trouble. Many of the people who had left the church were good givers and we could not pay the bills without their financial support. I silently prayed to God as this negative report was shared and asked God to show us the way out of this crisis.

God did move almost immediately as several new visitors began to come to church. Every week new people visited the church services. These visitors, unlike those who visited before the group of 20 left the church, came back and many of them became regular attendees and members. God had kept His promise and I was seeing a revival take place in the midst of an exodus from the church. This was my first experience of growth by subtraction.

During my 10 years as their pastor, I watched the Holy Spirit move in the Capac Churches until the average attendance of the two churches tripled to over 200. Many folks had come to know Jesus as Savior and become members of the churches. It appeared that the exodus of the folks from the church was necessary for the church to grow.

Within a few years, the churches were able to hire their own associate pastor to help with preaching, visitation and youth ministry. When the subject came up for discussion, I immediately suggested that the church hire Lisa Clark. She attended the Cole Church where I was serving when I was appointed to Capac. After several interviews "Pastor Lisa" was hired and served as my associate pastor for the next six years. As I write this, she is now the senior pastor of the 2 Capac churches and is doing a great job.

It was while I was pastor in Capac that I became a member of the Detroit Annual Conference and my ministerial credentials were officially restored. That was a great day as I knelt in prayer and Bishop Linda Lee prayed over me.

Following her prayer, Bishop Lee gave an invitation to the congregation of over 1,000 to respond to God's call to ministry. I was surprised when I saw Kathy kneel at the altar and begin to weep. I knelt next to her as she shared that she believed God was calling her to ministry. We prayed together asking God for His will to be done. I did not know then what amazing things God had planned for Kathy.

The following year, I was asked to become an advisory member of area ministry called "Love In The Name Of Christ" also known as "Love Inc.". Through a series of resignations, I unexpectedly found myself to be the President of the ministry. This was a tough position to be in as I found the ministry was broke and in debt to individuals as well as the Internal Revenue Service.

The Love Inc. board of directors wanted to know what we were going to do to save the ministry. I told them I needed to spend time in prayer and seek God's will concerning this situation. As I prayed over the next week, I sensed God giving me a plan to revive Love Inc. and move the organization to new levels of ministry.

I called an emergency board meeting and shared with the Love Inc. board that I believed God wanted us to hire Kathy, who had training in bookkeeping and finances, to get our financial records in order. The board accepted my recommendation and Kathy began working on the financial records the next day.

While Kathy was working on the records, I asked each board member to begin contacting our supporting churches. We made a special financial appeal to the area churches to help get us through this crisis. Churches from all over the area responded positively to our call for help and money began to flow into the Love Inc. treasury. Within a few months all bills were paid and we had a small balance in the bank. It was a miracle of God's grace and power that Love Inc. had survived and was thriving.

Kathy was hired by the board of directors of Love Inc. as the first executive director since the financial crisis began. The ministry had outgrown the area in the basement of a sponsoring church and Kathy knew we needed a new home for the ministry. She soon found an empty building owned by a local physician. After sharing her vision for Love Inc., with him, the physician donated the building. With the approval of the board of directors, Love Inc. moved into a new home. This building remains the home of Love Inc. until this day.

Kathy came to me one day and shared her vision of having a free medical clinic sponsored by Love Inc. The board and I agreed to pray with her about this new ministry. Over the next few months Kathy and I would share what God was saying to us concerning this major step. At breakfast one morning, I felt God saying, "It is time." I shared what I believed God was telling me and Kathy and I rejoiced that we had the go ahead.

The "Loving Hands Free Medical Clinic" was born. Within weeks, the free medical clinic was up and running with supplies being transported to a different area church each week in an old Boy Scout trailer. A treatment room was set up in each church and treatment was provided by doctors, nurse practitioners, and nurses. Many people have received free medical care and the Loving Hands Free Medical Clinic became the first free medical clinic under Love Inc. in the United States. It now has a beautiful, permanent spot at one of the Lapeer churches.

After ten years of ministry in Capac, I received a call that the Michigan area bishop had appointed me to two churches in the Flint District of the United Methodist Church. I was returning to the district where I had found Christ as my personal Savior forty years before. I was excited to return to my spiritual roots in the Flint, Michigan area.

My new appointment was to the Halsey and South Mundy United Methodist Churches in Grand Blanc Township ten miles south of Flint. Our new home was the parsonage of the churches located across the road from Genesys Hospital, a major trauma center in Genesee County.

Across the road from the parsonage was also a large senior citizen housing complex called Abbey Park. I began to pray for ministry opportunities at the Halsey, South Mundy, Genesys Hospital and the Abbey Park senior complex. God began to open doors and ministry began to flow from the churches as God's Spirit moved in the hearts of the church folks.

We started Bible studies at both churches, began a weekly Gospel Hymn sing at Abbey Park and I was placed on the clergy on-call list at the hospital. The Halsey Church started a bus ministry whereby the folks at Abbey Park are able to attend Sunday morning worship. I was excited about the ministries moving forward but God had more for Kathy and me to do.

One morning I arose early and was praying when God began to speak to me about Kathy's call to ministry. I believed it was time for her to begin the process of becoming a United Methodist pastor. I was hesitant to speak to her about this as I was unsure how she would respond. I heard Kathy stirring in the bedroom and I walked down the hallway to tell her what I thought God was saying to me on her behalf. She then told me that God had been speaking to her also, and the day before, she knew in her heart that it was time. She was waiting for confirmation that God was really calling her to be a pastor and that confirmation came through me.

This happened during my second year at the Halsey and South Mundy Churches, and Kathy was approved for ministry at our annual church conference. This was the first step in a long process that could take up to two years before Kathy would be assigned to serve a church as pastor. To our surprise, a month later Kathy was sent as a district superintendent assignment (DSA) to pastor the Lennon United Methodist Church, which was ten miles west of Flint, Michigan. Kathy began her pastoral ministry on December 1, 2007, and I had to learn to do ministry without her being beside me as my partner every Sunday.

We continued to live together in the Halsey and South Mundy Church parsonage. Kathy had to travel 23 miles each way to her new church each Sunday and I had to learn the totally new role as a pastor's spouse. There was much change in our lives, but God was faithful to see us through it all.

When the Halsey and South Mundy Churches found out that Kathy was being assigned to a church as pastor, they were shocked. One member told me that if he had known she was going to be leaving his church, he would not have voted for her to enter ministry. I believe many other people felt the same way. Kathy was loved by the Grand Blanc churches and they were very sad to have her assigned elsewhere.

We have worked hard to make this transition as easy as possible. Sometimes we preach at each other's churches and we try to attend special events together at all three churches. Over time, the change has become easier for all of us and God has blessed our ministries.

The challenges Kathy had to face in her new ministry were difficult, but we knew our God was greater than any challenge and He would see her through whatever was to come. The Lennon United Methodist Church had gone through a tough time, much like what had happened when we were in Capac. Many people had left the church under the previous pastor and those who stayed were hurt and some were angry about the events that had taken place.

Kathy was instructed by our district superintendent not to discuss what had happen in the past and concentrate only on moving forward. This proved very difficult as folks wanted to discuss the problems that led to the exodus from their church. Kathy was strong and over the next year she preached and encouraged the congregation to follow the example of the Apostle Paul. In Philippians 3:13 Paul said, "Forgetting those things that are behind and looking forward to those things that are ahead I press on toward the prize of the high calling of God in Christ Jesus." Kathy was determined to lead the church forward and not allow things to go backwards. She said God told her to "love the people and preach the Word in truth and He would take care of the rest."

During the next few years, the Lennon United Methodist Church congregation began to look forward as the hurts of the past found healing. Over time the church has found new dreams and has let go of the past hurts. The Lennon Church has grown spiritually while Kathy has been their pastor and I am so proud of the wonderful ministry she has had there over the last seven years.

One of the highlights of my forty years of ministry came during my time at the Halsey and South Mundy Churches. I was nominated for the Harry Denman Evangelism Award in the Detroit Annual Conference of the United Methodist Church. At the 2011 Annual Conference, I received the Award from our Michigan area bishop. At the award service, I had opportunity to speak to the thousand member annual conference. I took the opportunity to praise Jesus for saving me and bringing hope to my hopeless life and the lives of many in my family. I knew that without Jesus

I would probably not be alive and very possibly lost for all eternity. Praise God from whom all blessings flow.

During my nine years of ministry at the Halsey and South Mundy United Methodist Churches, I have had the privilege of working with my youngest brother, Don (Donny). Don and his wife, Beth, began to attend the South Mundy Church during my second year as pastor. Don had been in youth ministry for 20 years. He had recently resigned from a large church in our conference. Don and Beth quickly became involved in ministry with me and after a few months, Don was hired as Director of Ministries at both churches where he still serves today.

It was also during this time, that my son Stephen told me that he believed God was calling him into ministry. Shortly thereafter, he began the process to become a United Methodist pastor. I was thrilled and invited Stephen to the Halsey and South Mundy churches to preach and sing. The church folks loved Stephen and invited him back several times. In spite of his enthusiasm and ability to preach and sing beautifully, the process of entering ministry proved to be more difficult for Stephen than it had been for Kathy or me.

During the last 7 years, Don and I have led three building programs, seen many people come to Christ and have taken in many new church members. God has truly blessed our ministry together.

Recently we invited our brother Eddie to preach a tent revival at the Halsey church. We had a great revival meeting. The Phillips' brothers even did the special music for the closing service. We truly made a "joyful noise" to the Lord.

We do not know what the Lord has for us in the coming years, but what we do know is that God is always faithful when we love and trust Him. And may all who come behind us find us faithful.

CHAPTER 22

Welcome Back Home

Dedicated in Memory of

Stephen Paul Phillips	Donna Marie Princing
November 16, 1977-	January 8, 1933-
November 30, 2013	December 4, 2013

As November 2013 arrived, nothing seemed unusual. The Christmas shopping season began to move into high gear, the temperatures began to drop and leaves were falling from the trees. Our family began to make plans for Thanksgiving and Christmas. With four children and ten grandchildren, it had become increasingly difficult to get everyone in our family together in one place at the same time.

We were blessed as each of our four children and their spouses were working, our children and grandchildren were in good health. Our three churches were doing well. By all appearances, it would be a wonderful holiday season and I was even beginning to listen to Christmas music.

My youngest son, Stephen, was working as an over the road truck driver, driving from Michigan to California and back each week. I would call Stephen every week while he was driving during his shift between 6 p.m. and 6 a.m. We would talk about things he had seen in his travels. Recently I had inquired how he was feeling since having a serious bout with stomach problems earlier in the fall.

Stephen turned 36 on November 16, 2013. I called to wish him a Happy Birthday. He informed me that he was feeling better and had had a nice birthday. Then out of the blue Stephen told me something that shook me. He said, "Dad I think I am going to die." I was shocked and inquired as to why he would think such a thing.

Stephen told me of vivid dreams that he had been having in which he died. These dreams were so real, he had become very concerned about the safety of the truck he was driving and about his family. Stephen asked me, if he died, if I would make sure his boys, Gage and Braxtyn were taken care of.

I assured Stephen that I would take care of the boys but I did not believe anything was going to happen to him. I encouraged him to listen to Christian music, spend time in prayer as he drove home and we would talk more when he got home.

As soon as I finished my call with Stephen, I called his wife Karen. I told her of my conversation with Stephen. I asked her to get a doctor appointment for Stephen for Friday when he got home and she agreed. Stephen went to the doctor and had a complete checkup. The doctor found nothing wrong and he was back on the road.

That same week, Stephen posted a picture on his Facebook page that he had received on his birthday. It was a picture from his friend Brent that was taken on their 16th birthday. In the picture, Stephen was holding a cake which was decorated with the words "Happy Birthday Brent and Stephen-Drive Safe." Stephen wrote "Thanks Brent for the birthday picture. It's hard to believe it's been 20 years."

I was very relieved when Stephen called me to give me the doctor's test results. I tried to put out of my mind the concern that Stephen was going to die and returned to making plans for Thanksgiving and Christmas. I believed it was going to be a very happy holiday season for our family.

Thanksgiving Day was different that year, as only Sarah and her three children were coming for Thanksgiving dinner. Our other three kids had dinner plans with their in-laws or were beginning the tradition of staying home with their families. Kathy and I decided to take our daughter and grandchildren to work at a soup kitchen helping to serve Thanksgiving dinner. We had the privilege of helping to serve over 350 people and felt very blessed as we returned home in the late afternoon.

When we got home, Kathy put a turkey in the oven so we could have a small Thanksgiving family dinner. That evening, our daughter Stephanie arrived with two of our other grandchildren. The grandkids were going to spend the night to be with us all day on Friday as we followed our yearly tradition for the day after Thanksgiving.

Every year we invited our children and grandchildren to spend Thanksgiving night. On Friday morning, we started out at Chuck E Cheese for games and fun. We then had lunch at Ci Ci's Pizza and returned to the parsonage to decorate for Christmas. Then on Friday evening, Kathy and I invited all of our family to go to Crossroads Village located just north of Flint. There we would see a Christmas play, attend the annual Christmas tree lighting ceremony, ride the carousel and Ferris wheel and close out the evening riding the Huckleberry Railroad Christmas train.

When Stephen and his family arrived at Crossroads Village, I greeted them with hugs. We visited as we walked to the theater for the Christmas play. The remainder of the evening was so much fun. We laughed so much and had a great time. The memories of that evening will be a special blessing as long as I live.

When we got off the train at the end of the evening, I headed for the parking lot. I was scheduled to meet Stephanie to deliver her two children and I was running a little late. When I got to the parking lot, I realized that Stephen and his family were not with the rest of us. One of Stephen's boys had to go to the bathroom and we had gotten separated in the crowd.

I was upset that I had not said, "goodbye and I love you," as I always ended our visits and phone calls with those words. As we started driving towards the exit, I heard my granddaughter, Saige say, "Papa there they are!" I immediately turned around and drove to where Stephen and his family were standing on a small hill by a split rail fence that separated two parking lots. I said my goodbye and I love you and gave hugs to all. Stephen and his family responded likewise and I drove away into the night to deliver my grandchildren to my daughter.

Saturday was a busy day of preparation for Sunday services. It would be the first Sunday in advent so there were extra things to arrange and the day went by quickly. That evening, my good friend Gary Wright, from my God Squad days and his son Micah were to arrive at the parsonage. Our churches supported a Christmas project sponsored by Gary's ministry, World Renewal. We had collected bags of items called "Bundles of Hope" to be delivered to an orphanage in Haiti. Gary had come to give us a report about the ministry and to take the many bags of Christmas gifts to Indiana to be shipped to Haiti.

It was almost 10 p.m. when Gary arrived. We then enjoyed a very nice visit before heading to bed a little after 11 p.m.

Sometime near midnight, I awoke suddenly with a terrible pain in my stomach. It was unlike any pain I had ever felt and I wondered if something was seriously wrong with me. I sat in the living room and prayed for about thirty minutes. The pain slowly went away. I returned to bed and quickly fell asleep.

Sunday morning I was up at 6 a.m. to begin my Sunday morning routine of opening the Halsey Church, getting the church bulletins in place, checking the thermostat and heading for South Mundy church about 6 miles away. When I arrived, my brother, Don, and his wife, Beth, were there. We went over plans for the day's services as we waited for Gary to arrive.

Gary arrived at 8:15 a.m., fifteen minutes before the early service was to begin. When he walked through the door, he seemed different, as if something was wrong. He asked Don and me to come into the sanctuary. As we walked into the sanctuary he said, "I have some bad news. This is really bad." My immediate thought was that something had happened to one of the missionaries or the kids at the Haiti orphanage.

Gary asked Don and me to sit down and I commented, "This must be really bad."

It was then that Gary said, "Stephen was in a bad automobile accident last night."

I immediately responded, "My Stephen?"

Gary then said, "Yes and he didn't make it. I am so sorry."

As I heard those words, my world went into slow motion. I stood and began to try to find a place where I could be alone with God, as I said over and over, "Oh, God. Oh, God. Oh, God." I found a chair in the new Sunday school wing and I fell on my knees and began to weep uncontrollably.

I felt as if I was standing at the edge of an ocean and a monster wave had just hit me full force. I seemed to be spinning out of control. The sorrow I was feeling was so absolutely overwhelming. I covered my face, refusing to open my eyes, as I prayed that this was a bad dream. In my confused thinking, I thought that if I kept my eyes closed, this would continue to be a nightmare, but if I opened my eyes, it would be reality.

After several minutes, Don's wife Beth came and offered to take me home to Kathy. I finally opened my eyes, but I covered my face with both hands as we drove the 6 miles to the parsonage. When we arrived, I stumbled into Kathy's arms and we fell on our knees at the living room sofa.

As I wept, Kathy filled me in on what she knew of the accident. Stephen was alone in his car when it left the road less than a half mile from his home. The car went through a ditch and rolled several times in an open field. Stephen was thrown from the car to the spot where he died. As Kathy was filling me in on what had happened, the phone rang. Stephen's wife Karen was calling to tell us that she was on the way to Port Huron Hospital to identify Stephen's body. I immediately told Kathy, "We have to go the hospital". We got in the car as Kathy drove the 90 minutes to Port Huron Hospital, while I kept my face covered and cried.

As we traveled, I realized that we needed to call Sarah and let her know of this terrible tragedy. Obviously distraught, Sarah said she would be on her way from her home in Blissfield, Michigan, about a 90 minute drive to the parsonage and about 3 hours to the hospital. Sarah volunteered to call her mother to let her know what had happened.

Upon arrival at the Port Huron Hospital, before we were taken into a viewing room where Stephen's body was to be brought for identification, Kathy called Jason and asked him to call Stephanie. Jason said they would be on their way to be with us to help us through this terrible day.

Stephen's wife, Karen, was already there with her mother and Pastor Lisa Clark. Within minutes of our arrival, Stephen's mother arrived, followed by Jason and his wife, Karen, and Stephanie. Sarah was three hours away. There was no way she could get there in a timely manner, so she drove directly to the parsonage.

There were lots of tears, hugs and questions as we waited for the moment when I would help identify my son as the victim of a fatal automobile accident. We waited and waited and waited, but Stephen's body never arrived. We finally protested the long delay and were informed that we would not be allowed to see Stephen's body. It was a devastating blow to all of us. Only a picture was brought to the room for Karen to identify as being a picture of Stephen's body.

When the picture identification was over, I told Kathy, "I have to get out of here." We headed for the parking lot and Jason insisted on driving us home. My first priority though, was to go to Stephen's boys to try to comfort them. I knew how much they loved their dad and how much he loved them. I had to see them and hold them in their time of sorrow.

Jason drove us to the boys' other grandparent's home where they waited with their Grandpa Roger. Gage met us at the door. We embraced and wept together as I prayed for God's comfort to fill his heart. Next I found Braxtyn where he was playing a video game. I sat beside him, gave him a big hug and told him that Papa loved him so much. He just said, "I know" and then he said very calmly, "My daddy was killed in a car wreck and your son, too." I believe Braxtyn, in his own little boy way, was in shock and could not comprehend what was happening.

After staying for a while, Jason drove Kathy and me back to the parsonage in Grand Blanc where Sarah was waiting with her three children. We cried a lot that day as we tried to piece together what had happened to bring this awful event to pass. I could not get a grip on the facts. I felt that I needed to go to the accident scene so I could put into perspective what had happened. The initial report by someone was that Stephen had veered to miss a deer. I feared that if I didn't go to piece this together myself, I would regret it for the rest of my life.

On Monday afternoon, we traveled to Stephen and Karen's home. Sarah and her three children went with us. Since they love to be with their cousins, we also thought it would help Gage and Braxtyn to have them there to sooth their hurt.

Karen told us of the events from the time we had said goodbye at Crossroads Village on Friday night, until the police called Sunday morning.

Stephen had left the house about 10 p.m. on Saturday night and Karen went to bed. Gage said that he was awakened by sirens. He saw flashing lights sometime in the night but went back to sleep. He had no idea it had anything to do with his dad.

Early Sunday morning, a coworker called Karen from her workplace to tell her that the police were trying to find her. The police had been to the house the night before but, because the bedrooms were at the opposite end of the house, no one heard them knocking. Shortly after the call from work, the police called Karen and asked to come to the house to speak with her. Karen was very frightened by all that was happening and called to talk to Kathy.

It was not long after Karen called Kathy the first time, when a police officer arrived to notify Karen that Stephen had been killed in an automobile accident, less than one half mile south of their home. Karen then immediately called Kathy a second time telling her that Stephen had died. Gary Wright and his son Micah "just happened" to be at the parsonage when the calls came informing Kathy of Stephen's death. Gary comforted Kathy and prayed with her. He then volunteered to give me the worst news that I had ever received in my 63 years of life.

I thought Gary had come to give a mission's report and pick up some Christmas presents, but in reality, God had sent Gary because he was needed to comfort my wife and to inform me of Stephen's passing. Even in our darkest moments, God is watching over us, providing us with comfort and guidance.

After I listened to Karen's recollection of the events of Saturday night and Sunday morning, the big question became what happened that Stephen would drive off the road and roll his car? There were many theories about what happened but all we know for sure is that for some unknown reason Stephen's car left the road and Stephen was thrown from the rolling car and died.

I told everyone there at the house that I needed to go to the accident scene by myself, to spend time with God trying to make some sense of this event. In spite of pleas for me not to "go down there", I drove south just over a quarter mile. I parked my car where Stephen's car left the road. I could see where the car hit the ditch. I followed the debris field where the car had rolled, until I came to the spot where the car had stopped. I looked all around but I could find no sign that Stephen had been on the ground anywhere near where the car had stopped. I retraced my steps three times. I was about to give up when I heard God whisper, "Go further." I began to walk further south about 40 feet from the place where the car came to a rest. There I found a pool of blood where Stephen had died.

When I saw my son's blood soaking the ground, I fell on my knees. I cried out to God commending Stephen's soul to our Heavenly Father. I pled for mercy for Stephen and our family as we dealt with his loss. I returned to the house and to everyone's relief, I had not had a breakdown and was handling things well.

As I sat visiting with family members, I was struck with a very troubling thought. My son's blood was lying in a field, open to the elements or animals. Then I remembered what Mary the mother of Jesus did in the movie "The Passion of the Christ." Mary got rags and wiped up Jesus' blood so it was not trampled on by the Roman soldiers. I excused myself and I drove to the town of Yale a few miles away. I went to a store where I could buy some artificial flowers. I also purchased a plastic container where I could place the blood soaked soil from the accident scene. I returned to the house told Karen what I was doing and asked for a shovel. I went to the scene of the accident and dug up the red soil placing it in the plastic container which I put in my car. At the edge of the field, I planted the artificial flowers, piling rocks around the flowers so the winds of winter could not blow them away. I laid out more rocks in the shape of a cross to let all who passed by know that this was a place where someone went to Heaven.

I returned to the house and within minutes the phone rang. Karen entered into a conversation with the funeral director from Capac who was overseeing Stephen's funeral. I was stunned as I heard Karen begin to loudly sob. I went to her and asked what was wrong. She asked me to speak to the funeral director with whom I had done many funerals during my ten years in Capac. He informed me, as he had Karen, that Stephen's head was so badly damaged that it would be impossible to have an open casket at the funeral. He told me that in 60 years of funeral work he had never seen a person's head as damaged as Stephen's.

With this new blow to our hearts and hopes, we headed home to begin to try to get ready for Stephen's funeral. Over the next two days, I spent every spare minute working on a tribute that I could read at the funeral service. I could not sleep at night. I found myself writing and rewriting my tribute, wanting to say just the right things to describe my precious son.

On Wednesday night, before the day of visitation at the funeral home, I went to bed early. As I had each night since our tragedy, I began to cry, but that night I experienced something horrible. I was suddenly overtaken with an indescribable fear that Stephen did not make it to Heaven. A wave of fear flooded over me like I had never experienced, a sense of total desperation flooded my mind. I believe that the forces of evil were attacking me at a time of helplessness. All I could do was cry out to the Lord.

I begged God to give me a sign that Stephen was at peace and in His holy presence. In the midst of my outcry, Kathy came into the bedroom. She held me and prayed for me until I calmed down.

Just as I got control of my emotions and began to experience some peace, the phone rang. It was Kathy's sister and she was frantic. I handed the phone to Kathy who listened for a moment and said goodbye. She said to me, "We have to go." Kathy's mother had stopped breathing and the ambulance was on the way. We were told to meet the ambulance in Flint at McLaren Hospital, but as we sat in the waiting room for about 30 minutes, the ambulance never arrived. After searching through the emergency room and the ambulance bays trying to find Kathy's mother, a second phone call came telling us we needed to come to Kathy's parent's home.

Although we knew Ma was gone to Heaven, Kathy and I did not talk about it as we drove. When we arrived at the home, Ma was lying on the living room floor. The paramedics were unable to revive her. Kathy's Dad and two sisters surrounded Ma with tears of sorrow. Kathy quickly joined them in their tears. After a time of weeping, Kathy prayed the most beautiful prayer, thanking God for such a wonderful mother. She was a wonderful mother-in-law also, as she treated me as a son all the years I knew her.

The next day was December 5, 2013. It was the day of visitation for our son, Stephen, at the funeral home in Capac. It was also Kathy's 60th birthday. Kathy's Mom had passed away just 2 hours before her birthday. I was so overwhelmed by all that was happening that I had forgotten the prayer that I cried out to God the night before asking for assurance of Stephen's presence in Heaven.

Early that morning of visitation, Stephen's wife called me and told me that she had just received a text from a Christian coworker. She had to read it to me. Karen knew nothing of the struggle that I had gone through the night before, which made the text message even more meaningful to me.

I want to share with you what was in that text message.

"I was in the middle of a dream and when I blinked my eyes all I could see was dust, I try to wave it out of my face but it appears to be more like fog than anything. I try to adjust my eyes but nothing works. Finally, one more hard blink and I rub them. I open my eyes and everything is clear. But where am I? I start walking. Then all of a sudden 2 amazingly large white pillars are in sight. It looks like it has gold trimming all around it as well as something written on it. But I can't see for sure.

I don't know what to do. I'm in a sea of clouds and just see white for as far as I can see. Then I hear a little rumble and some voices. "What is that"? I say out loud. No one responds. The rumble and voices are getting louder they seem more excited than anything.

Then I see something. I look to my right and see someone walking towards the gate on my left side. Pretty big guy, even he looks confused as to where he is. As he keeps walking, he passes me and it's someone I only know from pictures. I fall to my knees as I see it is Stephen. I watch him walk to the gates and slowly the gates open up towards him. A shadow appears and I can't catch my breath. Is this really happening?! I see a man come out in a bright white glorious robe. It's Jesus. Stephen looks behind him and tries to run, it seems as though it just hit him where he is and what happened. He wasn't allowed to run. He just collapsed.

Jesus came past the gate bent down next to Stephen and wrapped both hands around Stephen's head. Jesus stayed there for quite some time. I could hear both weeping. I wanted to run, but I was frozen. I couldn't move anywhere. They both stand up and all I hear is "Welcome back Stephen."

They both start walking into the gated area where 2 more people were standing there waiting. They wrap their arms around Stephen.

Then there is a poof. My eyes are filled with dust again and I wake up."

I began to weep as Karen finished reading the text to me. I knew that God had heard my prayer and had answered it through a Christian sister who did not know Stephen died in an open field or of the massive head damage. I have found great assurance from this message that my son is in

Heaven with Jesus. I believe that I even know who the two people were who greeted him when he entered the gates of the heavenly city.

At the visitation, later that day, friends came from all over the area. Almost every church where I had served as pastor was represented. Hundreds of wonderful friends came to share their condolences, to let my family know we were loved and supported in prayer.

When word got out that Kathy's mother had passed away the night before, Kathy was surrounded by loving family and friends who helped her get through that very hard day. We have felt bad that we had to postpone our grieving over the loss of Ma, but we could only handle one thing at a time. We had to get through Stephen's funeral the next day. Then we could concentrate on Ma's visitation and funeral. "He giveth more grace when the burdens grow greater..."

The next day we got up early and left Grand Blanc for the funeral home in Capac. I was in such a state of mind that I felt like I was in a trance as we entered the church to begin the funeral service. Pastor Lisa Clark led the beautiful service which closed with my tribute and my good friend, Dan Hays, singing "Go Rest High On That Mountain."

I would like to share with you my tribute to Stephen that I read at the service as my brothers Ed and Don stood with me.

> *My Tribute To Stephen*
>
> *I would like to begin my tribute to my son Stephen Paul Phillips with words of gratitude to all of you who have prayed for our family, provided meals, sent cards and flowers or expressed your love and concern by words and tears. Thank you, thank you, thank you!!*
>
> *It has been my privilege for the last 36 years to be the father and very close friend of Stephen. As with any parent I have had many wonderful times that were filled with joy and laughter. There have also been some tough times. Through it all I can honestly say that it has never been boring to be Stephen's dad.*
>
> *I can remember Stephen's birth 36 years ago at the Lapeer Hospital. As I was putting on a gown to enter the room where Stephen was born I heard the doctor yell, "Get in here he's coming" and it has kind of been like that ever since.*
>
> *As a baby I nicked named Stephen "Tank" because he was so determined to plow through anything in his way whether it was a closed door, a footstool or the family dog. He would lower his little head and push until he moved it or someone moved it for him.*

At church people loved Stephen but he could be a rascal. I remember the Sunday he escaped from the church nursery and came flying down the center isle of the sanctuary during the choir special. His plan was to make a run across the platform and head out the side door but I caught him as he was running by me and I held him until the embarrassed nursery worker came to retrieve him.

When Stephen started school I knew that the first few days of every school year would a wrestling match to get Stephen out of the car and into the classroom with Stephen kicking and screaming all the way.

It wasn't that I did not discipline Stephen. He told me himself that he never got a spanking that he did not deserve and he got plenty of them. When I would give him a spanking he would look at me and say, "Go ahead and beat me some more I don't care." Once he told me, "Thanks Dad I really needed that." Stephen was the poster boy for the "Strong Willed Child."

Stephen always had lots of friends. He was just fun to be around. Whether at church or at school he was always very popular. But he did try my patience.

I took him to a camp meeting where I was preaching for 8 days when Stephen was 10 years old. One day an elderly minister, who just happened to be the camp treasurer, came to me and asked if I had a gun. I told him, "No." He then asked, "Does your boy have a gun?" I told him that Stephen did have a BB gun that he used to shoot at targets in the woods. He then informed me that Stephen had shot him in the buttocks. Stephen claimed that it was an accident but many years later he confessed that he did intentionally shoot the old minister in the buttocks.

I would have made him apologize but the old man had long since passed away. Needless to say, I was never invited to preach at that camp again.

As Stephen grew towards adulthood I began to see two sides to Stephen. There was the tough, serious side and there was the tender, fun side.

On the tough side-Stephen worked as a roofer from the time he was 20 years old to 31. He became stronger and more confident of his physical abilities and as a result he took that "Tank" attitude from childhood into his adult life. Stephen just did not back down from anyone or any challenge.

At our home on North Lake we have a neighbor who was a troublemaker for years. It got so bad that all the neighbors went to the Township police, the Sheriff's department and even went to the prosecuting attorney to try to stop the trouble this man was causing.

Nothing worked until the day he went after Stephen. It was everything I could do to keep Stephen from hurting the guy. After that confrontation the man left his house and did not return for three weeks. The troublemaking stopped and has never returned.

On the tender/fun side–Stephen could be the life of the party. His personality and sense of humor were infectious and he was just fun to be around. Someone wrote on Facebook that he would light up a room with fun and laughter.

Stephen had a great sense of humor. When the movie "Forest Gump" came out Stephen could quote from memory any spot in the movie and do it better than Tom Hanks. We would laugh so hard we'd cry.

Recently someone asked Stephen why he shaved his head. He responded, "It is because I have like 6 gray hairs on my scalp and I don't want to see any grays yet! Besides I don't think the wife would like all the attention I got with the curls!!"

On Facebook May 13th of this year Stephen wrote, "Holy crap! I just sneezed so hard I broke my belt and hit my forehead on the steering wheel which honked the horn! That's a 1-2 punch I didn't expect!"

Stephen's also had a soft and tender side and he would help anyone who was in need. In 2012 Stephen worked at the grocery store in Yale. He wrote on Facebook one day, "Yesterday when I was at work I had to help a young handicapped boy and his mother. When they were walking out I made sure the boy got a sticker and he responded like I gave him a PS3 or XBox by hugging me and saying thank you. There is no greater feeling than helping people and putting a smile on a child's face."

During Stephen's teen years we had many ups and downs but I will never forget the day he called and asked me to meet him at the Omard United Methodist Church where I was pastor in Brown City.

When I got to the church Stephen asked me to pray with him to receive Jesus as his Savior and to baptize him. That day made up for any problems that had taken place in the past. But

I soon found out that Stephen would have a spiritual struggle as difficult as any I have ever witnessed.

I have never known a person who was so torn between right and wrong. In Romans 7:15, Paul shared his struggle when he writes, "I don't really understand myself, for I want to do what is right, but I don't do it. Instead, I do what I hate…" 22, "I love God's law with all my heart but there is another power within me that is at war with my mind…In my mind I really want to obey God's law but because of my sinful nature I am a slave to sin." Jesus told Peter in Matthew 26:41, "Watch and pray for the spirit is willing but the flesh is weak." That was Stephen. He always desired to serve God but struggled so hard to get it done.

I remember many times when Stephen and I prayed for God's guidance for his life. Once he asked for spiritual help when he lived in Ypsilanti and I was far away. I called Rev. David Moulder who went and prayed all night with Stephen. I am forever grateful.

In 2001 Stephen took his Emmaus Walk and expressed at the closing that he believed God was calling him into ministry. That was an exciting day for me but as time went on Stephen continued to experience that war in his mind. My brother Don worked a Chrysalis Flight (Emmaus Walk for teenagers) with Stephen in 2004. Don said he and Stephen would talk into the early morning about his spiritual struggles and I believe it really helped.

Stephen's life took a very positive turn when on Christmas Eve 2005 he married Karen Chalmers right here at Zion Church in front of this Cross and next to this Christmas tree. I am wearing the tie I wore that night as I stood in the wedding party. That was a happy day. Gage became my grandson that night and it was a very merry Christmas for our family. I got a new daughter-in-law and grandson for Christmas that year.

In 2007 Braxtyn was born and Stephen's family was complete and very blessed. He was so proud of his wife and his handsome boys.

After a family crisis in 2011 Stephen began to earnestly seek ministry. He took both the United Methodist Lay Speaker Class and the Certified Lay Speaker Class in one month. I have never met anyone else who ever accomplished that task that fast. Stephen even spoke at the graduation service.

Stephen began preaching in 2012. He preached at both The Halsey and The South Mundy United Methodist Churches in Grand Blanc, The Lennon United Methodist Church, The Ruby United Methodist Church, The Durand United Methodist Church, The Caseville United Methodist Church The Otisville United Methodist Church, The Fostoria United Methodist Church, The West Deerfield United Methodist Church and The Romeo United Methodist Church. Stephen was invited back to several of these churches to preach and sing.

Stephen also had a beautiful singing voice. One day in 2011 while visiting me at the Halsey Church he asked me to come to the sanctuary for him to sing me a song. Stephen sang "Blessed Assurance" and I was stunned at how beautiful Stephen could sing. Later he sang "Thank You" to me and it made me cry. Pastor Lisa told me that Stephen sang "Thank you to her one Sunday morning. We recorded both songs and I listened to them on Wednesday morning and I cried again.

The process to become a pastor did not go well for Stephen and after waiting for a year with little response to his inquiries to enter ministry Stephen became discouraged and went back to driving a semi over the road.

Stephen was an excellent truck driver. He had one ticket in 5 years of driving because his load was loaded incorrectly. The company paid the ticket.

But truck driving was never Stephen's #1 choice of careers because he had to be away from his family so much and he knew God was calling him into ministry. He worked hard and experienced much loneliness being far from home because he knew he needed to take care of his family.

Stephen was so very excited about having 3 days off for Thanksgiving this year. He got a nice yearend bonus from work and was going to pay off all his bills and buy a second car. On the Friday after Thanksgiving our family always goes to Crossroads Village for the Christmas Tree Lighting, Christmas Play, fireworks, riding the Carrousel, the Ferris Wheel, and the Huckleberry Railroad Christmas Train. Before his family arrived Stephen told Karen he could not wait to hug the nieces and nephews. They teased him that night by calling him Aunt Stephen. He bought all the 7 nieces and nephews that were there that night a light saber and later got replacements when some of them got broken. We had a wonderful evening. There was so much laughter and fun.

Was Stephen perfect? No. Did he do some stupid things? Yes. If you never have done anything stupid I would like to meet you for I don't believe we have met.

Whenever Stephen and I spoke on the phone or in person we always parted with "Goodbye, I love you Son and I love you Dad." Last Friday we said our "Goodbye and I love yous" at Crossroads Village for the last time this side of Heaven.

On Facebook July 31ˢᵗ of this year Stephen wrote, "It's good to be home." I believe he would write the same thing today with maybe a hundred exclamation points for he is now at home in Heaven.

My Son rest in the arms of Jesus and I promise we will be together soon where there are no "Goodbyes"-only "I love Yous."

After the committal service and luncheon, we returned to the cemetery where my family gathered. We dug a hole where we buried the plastic container holding the blood stained earth from the accident scene along with some letters from Stephen's wife and boys. Stephen's body was cremated and his ashes sit in a beautiful container on the mantle of the fireplace in the home he loved so much.

Kathy had such a hard time at Stephen's funeral that Beth needed to take her home during the funeral dinner. Now it was time to begin to plan for her mother's funeral. Grieving for Ma was set aside to take care of details. It was decided by Kathy's family to have Ma's funeral service at the Halsey Church. Kathy's family had several family gatherings at the Halsey Community Center and it was a familiar environment. The church was full of family and friends when the service began on December 10, 2013. God blessed the service where Kathy gave a beautiful tribute to her Mom.

Part of what Kathy shared was the incredible courage her mother had displayed since their family car was hit by a drunk driver when Kathy was 9 years old. Ma was so badly injured in the accident that the doctors told her she may never walk again. Ma proved the doctors wrong. She went on to live a productive life as a loving mother and wonderful wife to Kathy's dad for 61 years. This union brought forth four children. Kathy was the firstborn. She was followed by her brother Jeff, her sisters Julie and Dawn.

The following is my wife Kathy's tribute to her mother:

On Sunday night, December 1, 2014, I shared with my Mom on the phone our terrible loss in the death of Stephen in a car accident. I explained to her that I would not be visiting that week as we would be so busy preparing a funeral and housing family from out of town and I understood that she would not be able to attend the funeral service. But when I awoke that Wednesday morning of December 4th, I just sensed that I needed to go to her. When I arrived after lunch, Dad told me that Mom couldn't get out of bed today, but he knew she would want to see me. I went into her room and gently awakened her. She began to cry and reached out to comfort me, and we cried together. She asked me so many questions that day about the accident and Stephen – and about Heaven. Then, I climbed in bed with her and held her for a while and it felt so good. When it was time for me to leave, she insisted on getting up. I tried to argue with her that she was in too much pain for that and she said to me, "Well, you can help me." I did - - and she did. The three of us, Mom, Dad and me, visited for a while more before I hugged and kissed them both goodbye and told them I loved them. Little did I know, but that would be the last time, this side of Heaven.

MEMORIAL TRIBUTE READ AT THE SERVICE FOR MAMA.

Our mother was "one in a million." She was full of surprises right up to the end of her earthly life. How many times over the last 10 years have we thought Mom would be leaving us – and then she would rally – and give us some more time because we needed her here. I think she had some kind of pull with the Heavenly Father that way.

Our mother was a great athlete in High School and those friends and family who have known her many years can attest to that. She should have been inducted into the Flint Athletes Hall of Fame just as my dad and Uncle Bill were a few years back. Mom played infield and pitched on the Beecher Buccaneer's softball team and they were contenders in their division. She always wanted to be able to pitch "windmill" but told me her shoulder just would not pivot that way – but was so proud of her great-granddaughter Lauren for her *accomplishments in perfecting that windmill pitching style. Mom told us of her softball coach, Russ Reynolds, who always put the bunt sign on for her when she came to bat with men (girls) on base. She begged him to let her swing away and then she would pop out. "Pop out, pop out, pop out" Mr. Reynolds would say. "Next time you'll bunt!" And then she would beg to swing away. Mom had a very competitive spirit and it came out in many ways. Mom continued to play softball long after high school.   She also was a great high school basketball player for a 5'2" gal. We actually have a picture of her "reverse – dunking" the basketball – at least that was her story. Mom was very competitive and she even added Field Hockey and track to her repertoire. She was a natural athlete as were both of her little brothers, John and Dan. Whatever we were doing – from board games to card games to shooting hoops in the driveway – our mom was competitive – I think much like her mother before her as I remember some of those games of spoons we played as kids with Gramma Boulton! Dad told me a couple years ago that Mom and the Boulton boys had such natural athletic gifts that they didn't have to work very hard to improve. He on the other hand, had to spend hours at practice to compete. Do you think any of us inherited that competitive nature of our parents?*

July 4th 1962, forever changed our mom's life and our families' life. We were on our way to Uncle Dale and Aunt Lois' cottage at Otter Lake for a 4th of July picnic when a drunk driver caused a 3 car crash on M-15. One person in the 2nd car was killed and our mother was busted up very badly. The 2 drunk people who caused the accident walked away with a few cuts. Mom's hip was crushed; she had broken ribs, a huge gash on her forehead and a concussion. She was holding Julie in the front seat (in those days baby car seats were not a requirement), but she shielded Julie with her own body to save her life. Jeff and I were in the back seat and were tossed around with a few abrasions. Dad had tried desperately to steer out of the on-coming 2nd car which hit us head-on and the steering wheel actually broke off the column in his effort to save all of us. One year old Julie was badly bruised because of the pressure mom had gripped her with. The doctors thought mom may never walk again. HA! He didn't know that competitive spirit of hers. Several weeks later after surgery and therapy, mom walked out of that hospital on crutches. But the severity of those injuries would forever more plaque her with a life of pain. No more sports. That part of her life was now in the past.

As the years went on and the pain continued, mom did the best she could. She had a long career working first for Beecher Plaza Drugs on Coldwater Rd. in Beecher and later at Flushing Pharmacy in Flushing. She pushed through the pain to help provide some extras for our family – who by 1965 had added a baby sister, Dawn. Mom coached Jeff's little league baseball team for several summers. In those days, they played games during the day and dad was working hard at the A.C. Mom stepped in for him. And she could be feisty – because of that competitive nature. Have any of us inherited that?

Mom taught us all to give our best effort and do our best work – and I can remember nights she would get home from a 5 hour shift on her feet and hurt so badly. But she did what needed to be done for her family. She worked through the pain.

Our mom could cook some good food! She was an excellent cook and Dawn has inherited that gift. We always knew when we went over to her house there would be some kind of "left-over" in the fridge and mom's left-overs were better than any restaurant main course. Even though she was in pain, she'd stand at that stove and cook – because she knew we liked to eat! Thanksgiving Days were a feast to remember! And nobody makes pancakes like mom.

Mom had many talents that she never allowed herself to be praised for. She could do crafts, crochet the most beautiful afghans, and paint scenery pictures. She loved word search puzzles and regular puzzles. But most of all she loved my dad and her family.

Jeff, Julie, Dawn and I had no doubt that our mother loved us and sacrificed for us. She would go without new clothes so we had all we needed. She kept our clothes clean, our house clean, our meals cooked, helped with homework (and the "new math" drove her crazy!). She had a mother's heart and taught us girls to have the same – unselfish, sacrificial, unconditional love.

As the years went on, her pain intensified. She had several back surgeries and hip surgeries. Nothing seemed to give much relief. Depression began to take over and her joy for life began to dwindle. That was hard to witness. And oh, boy, did we all try to bring her out of that and make her laugh! Mon's sense of humor was "interesting." As a family we would sit around and watch comedies like Red Skelton, the Smother's Brothers and Laugh-in. We would all be cracking up - - and mom would say to us, "I don't know how you can laugh at that. They are stupid. Why I wouldn't even walk across the street to see that Tommy Smothers if he was laying in the ditch!" What did that mean????? She would have us rolling on the floor with laughter. She once said our family could have more fun sitting together in the living room doing nothing and laughing at nothing – and we did. Number 3!!!! Any of us that inherited that great sense of humor - - we got it from dad!! But every once in a while – we could get Mom laughing with us until she cried and almost wet her pants. Several of our vacations proved to be joyous occasions of mom's laughter as we could find ourselves in the funniest of situations. And there was the time Julie, Mom, and I decided to take a water aerobics class. I think we may have been kicked out after the first week because we laughed too much. Our mom was so "buoyant" that if she lifted one foot up – she just began to float. It was the most hilarious thing Julie and I ever saw. Most of the other women did not see the humor in it at all.

Mom's memory was stellar. She could remember things that most of the rest of us had forgotten long ago. Jeff inherited that from mom. We had a wonderful trip together 2 years ago and mom remembered where every family member used to live when she was a child – even if there was no longer a house on the property. And just recently, she sang us the Chiquita banana song from memory – all 3 verses!

When each of her grandchildren came along, she was so proud and she spoiled you all. Of course my kids were born well before my siblings' children – because I inherited that competitive spirit and had to be first. But Jason, Stephanie, Ben, Josh, Tyler, Jesi, Sidra, Sam, Sarah and Stephen - - your grandma loved each one of you so much and was so very proud of you. And I know all of you loved her. Draw from her inner strength to keep going even when things get tough – just like she taught us. Work through your pain and love unconditionally.

And then how proud she was to have these beautiful and perfect great-grandkids: Ryan, Gage, Gavin, Isaac, Lauren, Saige, Phillip, Easton, KayLiegh, Braxtyn, Levi, Eden,

Brinleigh, Weston, Matthew, Chloe and Cody. She loved
having you around her to help her get her mind off her pain
for a while. Great – Gramma (or Aggie as Matthew called her
and Gramma Footprints as Josh's boys called her) always had
LOTS of candy and ice cream around, didn't she? You all were
so important to her and she was so proud of you! She said more
than once, "We don't have one homely kid in our whole family!"

Our parents were married 61 years and theirs is a love
story that movies are made. They loved each other through thick
and thin and in my 60 years, I NEVER heard words of anger
directed at each other. Theirs was a love built on respect for one
another and unconditional commitment. Dad, you and mom
have been an exemplary example for each one of us to follow.
You did begin to crack us up though, Dad, when you both
began to lose your hearing. There were some very interesting
conversations going on in that house! And even through that
frustration, you helped mom remember how to laugh things off.
Dad, you took such good care of mom and NEVER gave up
hope that one day she would be well again – to enjoy life with
you and all of us. Thank you, dad, for loving our mom in such
a tender and complete way.

These last couple years have been difficult for mom and
she got tired of the fight to live on. She and I had several
conversations about heaven in the last months. She would say
to me, "I hope God will accept me." And I would tell her that
because of her commitment to Jesus Christ, God was already
preparing a place for her to abide with HIM forever. She
wanted it to be sooner than later and I would tell her that
God's timing is perfect. She longed for that place where there
is no more pain and no more sorrow and no more worry or
tears. She longed for that place where she would dwell with
her Savior – and she would have a new body (a thin one, she
hoped) and she would be able to sing with a beautiful voice.

I spent nearly 3 hours with mom and dad on Wed.
afternoon. Mom was in horrendous pain, yet she got out of
bed and sat with dad and me for a while. On Wednesday
evening, the angels came. My sisters and my dad did all they
could to revive mom once more – but God's timing is perfect
and God knew the desire of mom's heart. Even though she
hated to leave all of us behind here – she was ready to go. And
you better believe that she will be waiting at that gate for our

arrival – in God's perfect timing. Until then, she has many loved ones to catch up with: Uncle John and Aunt Pat, friends and loved ones – precious tiny grandbabies to rock - and now Hal's and my son Stephen. But most of all – her Lord and Savior Jesus Christ.

Family and friends – don't miss out spending eternity with our mom in heaven. God's Word tells us that we must be born again by the spirit. Jesus Christ is our ticket to heaven. We can never be good enough to get there on our own. Jesus gave His life – to save ours – just like our mom nearly gave hers to save Julie's in the car accident. We don't know when it will be our day to be here --- at a service like this. This is our second service for a family member in 4 days. Our decision about eternity must be made before our time on this earth is up. Our mom, your grandma, your great-grandma, your sister, your aunt, your friend – she knew that. And in that competitive nature of hers - - she beat us all there!

Until we meet on the other side – Mama, we love you and we thank you for loving us.

We had entered in to our "great time of sadness," but through the grace of God, we were able to rise out of the ashes once again. Folks, during times like this, a surface faith will not cut it. We need a deeply rooted faith that can stand strong in the time of storms. What would I have done without my Jesus? - Kathy Phillips

For 40 years I have begun funeral services with this prayer, "O God our Father from whom we come at the time of our conception and to whom we go at the time of our death, we pray that You would grant us the divine favor of Your loving presence at this time in our earthly lives."

When Jesus spoke to Stephen in the beautiful dream, I believe Jesus was confirming that we come from God and we return to God. I believe that both my son and my mother-in-law heard those precious words from our Savior, "Welcome Back Home."

CHAPTER 23

Our Hope

As I begin this last chapter, it has been ten months since we entered our great time of loss. Following the funerals, we tried to get back in the spirit of Christmas but nothing was the same. Our great loss turned to a great sadness that seemed to hang over our heads like a dark cloud.

Almost every night for the first month, I cried myself to sleep. Sometimes I felt that I could not breathe as the grief seemed suffocating. There were days when I thought I would die. Other days I would feel God's blessing flowing over me in wonderful peace. My roller coaster emotions only seemed to even out after months of weeping, praying and studying God's Word.

There was a time when I prayed to God to let me die so I could get out of the intense pain I was experiencing. Yet through it all, I continued my pastoral ministries visiting sick people, encouraging the discouraged and preaching the Gospel. I never missed a service during the first two months after Stephen and Ma died.

Some of my pastor friends advised me to take a month off and just rest. I knew if I did, I would have an even rougher time. I had to keep busy to keep from thinking about my son and mother-in-law. If I did not stay busy, I would find myself breaking down and sobbing. It was so hard but by God's grace Kathy and I kept going, holding on to each other.

Following the funerals, Kathy and I both got sick. A combination of exhaustion and changes in weather led to sinus infections and bronchitis. My doctor was very kind as I shared all that had happened. Within a few weeks, I was healthy again.

Michigan weather was beginning to turn very cold. Just before Christmas, our area was hit with one of the worst ice storms in Michigan history. When Christmas Eve arrived, we were in the midst of a massive power outage. Of our three churches, South Mundy Church was the only one that had electricity. We had to cancel the Christmas Eve services at the Halsey and Lennon Churches.

I had a wall heating unit that kept the parsonage warm enough to allow us to stay home and not have to go to a motel. Our daughter, Sarah, and her children came for Christmas and we all spent Christmas Eve and Christmas morning in candle and lantern light. The grandkids told me it was a Christmas they would never forget. It was my first Christmas without electricity in my 63 years of life. I hope it will be the last.

Through December, January and February, the cold continued with little relief. The snowfall was also unusually heavy. With everything else that had happened, this was soon becoming the worst winter of my life. I battled depression and had to tell myself every day that things were going to get better. I believed that if I just held on, the pain of grief would let up and I would be able to close my eyes without tears beginning to fall.

Kathy and I have taken a mid-winter trip to Florida for many years. It provides us a two week break from the cold and a time to rest from the pressures of ministry. While in Florida we attend a camp meeting where we can hear Bible teaching and preaching. As we planned our 2014 winter trip, we were especially looking forward to spending time in the warmth of Florida and basking in the warmth of God's healing grace. We also hoped to escape the great sadness.

Our trip was very nice, as we received some much needed down time. We also heard some great preaching and teaching at The Florida Holiness Camp in Lakeland, Florida. From camp meeting, we took a 5 day cruise to the Caribbean. We had a nice time but even in paradise, the great sadness still had a hold on us. As we came to our last weekend in Florida, I preached in a Free Methodist Church in Bradenton, Florida. I had met the pastor when I was a Free Methodist evangelist in the 1980s. We reconnected the year before and he invited me to come and preach for him on our 2014 trip.

The service went well, the pastor was welcoming and the folks were very friendly. Many of the people were United Methodists from Michigan who knew people from our churches at home. Several of the folks knew my brother Eddie. Some had had him stay in their homes when he traveled.

As we headed north on I-75 toward Michigan on that Sunday afternoon, I was disappointed that I had not had the healing that I had hoped for. I was heading home with the dark cloud still hanging over me. I felt that I could begin to cry at any moment.

I never understood the pain of losing a child until it happened to me. The intense grief is unlike anything I have ever experienced. Even the worst times in my life did not compare to this emotional pain.

I felt badly that I had not done more for those I had served as pastor, who had lost their own child. I wondered if the pain would ever let up.

As I drove hour after hour, I prayed silently that God would show me how to go back and deal with the places and faces that reminded me of what Kathy and I had been through. There was a sense of dread, not just because of the extremely cold weather, but because we were returning to the "place of grief" back home.

We stopped for the night at a motel in northern Georgia and planned to drive the rest of the way home the following day. We had a plan, but God had another plan. When we neared Lexington, Kentucky the following afternoon, Kathy asked me to stop so she could take a break. When she returned to the car she informed me that she was sick and needed to find a place to go to bed.

We drove a few miles to a Lexington exit and found a motel near the expressway. Kathy told me she was going to take a nap, hoping that she would feel better when she awoke.

After I got her settled in at the motel, I felt strongly that I was to take a drive to the campus of Asbury University. It was there that I had experienced the greatest outpouring of God's Holy Spirit in my lifetime. I thought that maybe I would experience God's presence in a fresh and new way that could bring healing to my broken heart.

I drove the twenty miles to the campus. When I arrived at the campus, I immediately walked to Hughes Auditorium where the great 1970 Asbury Revival began and where I had my graduation ceremony in 1973. I thought this would be a great place to be alone with God, seeking comfort and strength before returning home to Michigan. When I got to Hughes Auditorium, I was disappointed as two men were setting up sound equipment for some upcoming event. I wanted to be alone with God.

As I left the auditorium, my eyes immediately went to a little white house that was the "Original Asbury College" built in 1890, by the founder of the college. In the upstairs of the little two-story building was a prayer chapel. I had used this prayer chapel many times during my college days. I remember there were always index cards with all kinds of prayer requests spread across the knelling altar. Many students and college staff used that altar through the years to carry their burdens to the Lord.

I climbed the stairs and found to my delight that in contrast to the cold outside, the chapel was very warm. I sat down in a chair that faced the altar and began a conversation with God. That conversation soon became like nothing I had ever experienced. God came to that little chapel. He spoke to me in a new and sometimes frightening way. I have referred to this experience as my "Shack" experience after the very popular book by the same name.

I shared with God my hurt, my anger, my regrets, my disappointment and my fears for the future. I told God I was hurting deeply and that I did not think I could go on in the same state of mind I had been in for the previous three months.

As crazy as it may sound, I believe God asked me what I wanted Him to do. I very honestly told God that if I had to live in the pain I was experiencing, I wanted Him to take me to Heaven. I did not want to live in this terrible pain anymore. I wept as God and I had an extremely intimate discussion about my future.

My only disappointment with the prayer chapel was that there was not a tissue to be found. I ended up finding an old piece of cloth behind the altar and used it to blow my nose over and over.

It was toward the end of this very unusual hour long conversation with my Lord that I believe God said, "OK, I will take you home. But I want you to think about what your death will do to your wife, children and grandchildren. What will your passing do to their trust in Me?"

That question stopped me in my tracks as I imagined my family receiving word of my death just a few months after Stephen and Ma's passing. I could imagine the devastation that another unexpected death would bring to those whom I loved the most.

I was silent for a while as I reconsidered my request to leave this world and join my son and mother-in-law in Heaven. When I did speak again, my attitude was different. The realization hit me very hard that my request would result in happiness for me, but so much sadness for my loved ones. When I spoke out loud again, my request had changed. I was now asking God to help me and my family to have peace in the midst of our pain and confusion.

God has answered that prayer in a powerful way over the last six months. I felt a burden lift from me there in that prayer chapel that has not returned.

I did have one more request of the Lord before I left the little prayer chapel. I asked that as soon as the time was right, when it would result in the greatest good for my family and the Kingdom of God that God would allow me to come home to Heaven. I sensed that God said, "We'll talk about that when the time comes."

I left the prayer chapel and drove back to Lexington to tell Kathy about my "Shack" experience. When I arrived at the motel, I found that God had been meeting with Kathy also. She shared that she had slept for several hours and when she awoke, God came to her at the motel bringing peace to her heart. She believed she was now ready to go home to move forward with her life and ministry. We held each other and prayed together. We thanked God that "He had a better plan." God's timing is perfect and we had just experienced a perfect example.

When we returned home the weather was still very cold, the snow was very deep but my heart was different. I had a peace I had not experienced since before Thanksgiving. Even though I still have my times of tears and sorrow, nothing is like what I was experiencing before my talk with God at Asbury.

Epilogue

October 2014

I now live each day with a fresh assurance that whatever I face My God is near and will not let me be defeated by the enemy of my soul. Kathy and I have a closer relationship than ever before as we continue to serve God at our three churches. We look forward to years of continued service before it is time to join our loved ones in Heaven with Jesus. Our hope is in the Lord Jesus and His resurrection power.

I trust that in the remaining years of my life and ministry, I will experience many more wonderful outpourings of God's presence. I hope to be able to write many more chapters about miracles and ministries that God might give to a guy who was saved From The Doors Of An Orphanage to serve the King of Kings and Lord of Lords. Praise the Name of Jesus.

I am serving in my 9th year as pastor of the Halsey and South Mundy United Methodist Churches in Grand Blanc, Michigan.

My wife Kathy is serving in her 7th year as pastor of the Lennon United Methodist Church in Lennon, Michigan.

My brother, Don, continues to serve with me as Director of Ministries at the Halsey and South Mundy United Methodist Churches. He lives with his wife, Beth, in Swartz Creek, Michigan.

My brother, Eddie, serves as a Free Methodist Evangelist. He lives with his wife, Karen, in Flushing, Michigan.

My sister, Julie, and her husband, Donald, are retired from ministry in the Church of Christ. They live in Maumelle, Arkansas.

Our children Jason, Sarah and Stephanie all love the Lord and attend church regularly with their families.

Stephen's widow, Karen, has returned to nursing school. She is working to become a registered nurse. She continues to live near Yale, Michigan, and attends church with her boys with Pastor Lisa in Capac, Michigan.

Our 10 grandchildren, Ryan (17), Gage (15), Gavin (15), Isaac (12), Lauren (12), Saige (12), Phillip (9), Easton (9), Braxtyn (7) and Eden (6), are growing up in Christian homes and love Jesus. I have been blessed to be able to baptize most of them.

Many things change as life goes on and we are finding our "new normal." I am so glad that the Jesus we serve is the same yesterday, today, and forever. People change, circumstances change, but Jesus is always the same. I have never regretted giving my heart to Jesus. My greatest desire is to help others to know Him as their Savior.

Please pass this book on to someone who needs to hear of God's saving grace. Please pray for our family and our ministry as we attempt to reach others with the message of God's love.

May God richly bless your life!
Pastor Hal Phillips